Authoritarian states
Study and Revision Guide

PAPER 2

Paul Grace

Authoritarian states

Study and Revision Guide

PAPER 2

Paul Grace

Every effort has been made to trace all copyright holders, but if any have been inadvertently overlooked, the Publishers will be pleased to make the necessary arrangements at the first opportunity.

Although every effort has been made to ensure that website addresses are correct at time of going to press, Hodder Education cannot be held responsible for the content of any website mentioned in this book. It is sometimes possible to find a relocated web page by typing in the address of the home page for a website in the URL window of your browser.

Hachette UK's policy is to use papers that are natural, renewable and recyclable products and made from wood grown in well-managed forests and other controlled sources. The logging and manufacturing processes are expected to conform to the environmental regulations of the country of origin.

Orders: please contact Hachette UK Distribution, Hely Hutchinson Centre, Milton Road, Didcot, Oxfordshire, OX11 7HH. Telephone: +44 (0)1235 827827. Email education@hachette.co.uk Lines are open from 9 a.m. to 5 p.m., Monday to Friday. You can also order through our website: www.hoddereducation.com

ISBN: 978 1 510432369

© Paul Grace 2018

First published 2018 by
Hodder Education
An Hachette UK Company
Carmelite House
50 Victoria Embankment
London EC4Y 0DZ

www.hoddereducation.com

Impression number   10 9 8 7 6 5 4

Year   2023

All rights reserved. Apart from any use permitted under UK copyright law, no part of this publication may be reproduced or transmitted in any form or by any means, electronic or mechanical, including photocopying and recording, or held within any information storage and retrieval system, without permission in writing from the publisher or under licence from the Copyright Licensing Agency Limited. Further details of such licences (for reprographic reproduction) may be obtained from the Copyright Licensing Agency Limited, www.cla.co.uk

Cover photo: © Bibliotheque Nationale, Paris, France/Archives Charmet/Bridgeman Images
Produced and typeset in Goudy and Frutiger by Gray Publishing, Tunbridge Wells
Printed and bound by CPI Group (UK) Ltd, Croydon, CR0 4YY
A catalogue record for this title is available from the British Library

Contents

How to use this book 5

Getting to know the exam 6

1 Authoritarian states 8
- Overview of authoritarian states 8

2 The USSR under Joseph Stalin, 1924–53 10
- The establishment of the Soviet Union and Stalin's rise to power 10
- Stalin's consolidation and maintenance of power 18
- Stalin's domestic policies: aims and results 24
- Exam focus 28

3 Germany under Adolf Hitler, 1933–45 30
- Hitler's rise to power 30
- Hitler's consolidation and maintenance of power 40
- Hitler's domestic policies: aims and results 48
- Exam focus 56

4 China under Mao Zedong, 1949–76 58
- Mao's rise to power 58
- Mao's consolidation and maintenance of power 66
- Mao's domestic policies: aims and results 70
- Exam focus 76

5 Cuba under Fidel Castro, 1959–2006 78
- Castro's rise to power 78
- Castro's consolidation and maintenance of power 86
- Castro's domestic policies: aims and results 96
- Exam focus 100

6 Argentina under Juan Perón, 1946–74 — 102
- Perón's rise to power — 102
- Perón's domestic policies: aims and results — 110
- Life in Argentina under the rule of Perón — 118
- Exam focus — 122

Glossary — 124

Key figures — 132

Timeline — 135

Answers — 137

How to use this book

- Welcome to the *Access to History for the IB Diploma: Authoritarian states: Study and Revision Guide*. This book has been written and designed to help you develop the knowledge and skills necessary to succeed in the Paper 2 examination. The book is organized into double-page spreads.
- Each double-page spread contains a summary of the key content you will need to learn and exam-focused activities related to and testing this content.
- Words in bold in the key content are defined in the glossary and key figures list (see pages 124–34).
- The exam-focused activities include Paper 2 exam-style questions so that you can develop your essay-writing skills. Answers for some activities can be found at the back of the book.
- At the end of each chapter, you will find an exam focus section. Here, you will find guidance on the History Paper 2 exam and the essay structure, as well as a checklist designed to help you write a successful essay. You will also find specific guidance and student answer examples with examiner commentary and annotations to help you to understand how to improve your grades.

Together, these two strands of the book will provide you with the knowledge and skills essential for examination success.

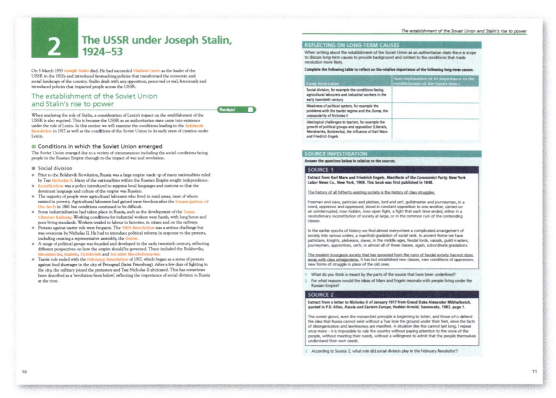

Key historical content   Exam-focused activities

At the end of the book, you will find:

- Glossary, Key figures and Timeline – key terms in the book are defined, key figures are highlighted and key dates are included in a timeline.
- Answers for the exam-focused activities.

Getting to know the exam

■ Types of questions

Paper 2 requires you to write two essays, each from a different topic. There will be a choice of two questions for each topic. You should answer only one of these questions for Topic 10: Authoritarian states and a second question for the other topic you have studied. Questions for Topic 10 may address:

- the emergence of authoritarian states
- the methods used to consolidate and maintain power in authoritarian states
- the aims and results of domestic policies.

■ Command terms

A key to success is to understand the demands of the question. Questions use key terms and phrases known as command terms.

Command term	Description
Compare	• **Discuss** the **similarities** of leaders, referring to both throughout your answer and not treating each separately • You should not give an overview of each leader and should focus on the most **important similarities**, rather than every tiny detail
Compare and contrast	• **Discuss** the **similarities and differences** of leaders, referring to both throughout your answer and not treating each separately • You should not give an overview of each leader and should focus on the most **important similarities and differences**, rather than every tiny detail
Contrast	• **Discuss** the **differences** between leaders, referring to both throughout your answer and not treating each separately • You should not give an overview of each leader and should focus on the most **important differences**, rather than every tiny detail
Discuss	• **Review various arguments** regarding a leader or leaders and conclude with an argument **supported by evidence**
Evaluate	• **Make a judgement** based on how strong or weak evidence may be
Examine	• **Analyse** the **strengths and weaknesses** of various arguments with a **concluding opinion**
To what extent	• **Determine the extent to which something is true or false**, with answers usually being 'to no extent', 'to some extent' or 'to a great extent'

■ Answering questions

- You will have five minutes of reading time at the start of the examination. It is during this time that you should review the questions in the two or more topics you have studied.
- Once you have identified which ones you are able to address, choose the Topic 10 question for which you have the most knowledge and whose demands you fully understand.
- Many students may have great knowledge regarding one or more authoritarian states or leaders, but they may not understand fully what the question wants them to do. If you find the wording of a question confusing, consider addressing another question if you feel more comfortable doing so.
- Once you have chosen your question for Topic 10, you should look at your other topic of study and repeat this exercise.
- Once you have made a decision on your second question for Paper 2, return to your Topic 10 question and begin to think about how you will address it, waiting for the end of the reading time.

Marks

All questions on Paper 2 are worth 15 points each for a total of 30 possible points for this Paper. In order to attain the highest mark band (13–15), your essays should include:

- answers that clearly address the demands of the question and are well structured and clear
- correct, relevant historical knowledge used appropriately to support your argument
- evidence that is critically analysed
- historical events that are placed in their context
- evidence that you understand there are different historical interpretations.

Timing your writing

- You will have 1 hour 30 minutes to complete both Paper 2 essays. This breaks down to 45 minutes per essay on average.
- Part of your writing time, however, should be spent preparing a basic outline which will help you keep your answer structured and focused.
- You should spend perhaps five minutes on this.

Defining your terms

It is important that you define the terms you use in the introduction of your essay.

If the question asks you:	Be sure to …
• about some political ideology	• explain what that ideology means
• to discuss two rulers, each from a different region	• state clearly the region the rulers are from
• to discuss propaganda	• explain what propaganda is and what formats you will address, such as radio, posters, cinema, or perhaps even education policy

Making an argument

- Your essays should make an argument, not just repeat details about a leader and their rule.
- Your argument should be stated explicitly in your essay's introduction and conclusion, with the supportive evidence discussed in the body of the essay.
- To strengthen your argument, use a range of supporting evidence. This evidence should be explained and connected to the question.
- Try to bring in conceptual understandings and historical comparison points within your writing to increase the sophistication of your analysis and evaluation.
- Higher-level responses will also discuss different perspectives. These could include the views of historians, opinions from the time period in question and your own interpretations. An evaluation of perspectives is required to reach the 13–15 mark band.

Good luck with your studies and the exam!

1 Authoritarian states

Overview of authoritarian states

Revised

The twentieth century saw the emergence of a wide range of authoritarian states. In this book we will review five case studies of authoritarian states under the following leaders:

- Joseph Stalin
- Adolf Hitler
- Mao Zedong
- Fidel Castro
- Juan Perón.

It is recommended that in preparation for your Paper 2 examination you study at least *three* authoritarian states. Some questions may ask you to compare states so it is helpful to be able to draw ideas from different case studies. Essay questions on Paper 2 are focused on three areas, which will be explained below.

■ The emergence of authoritarian states

This section explores the factors that allowed these states to come into existence. Studying for this should focus on the relative importance of conditions and methods.

Conditions refer to the existing situation in the country that may have aided the creation and establishment of an authoritarian state. For example, the economic depression played an important role in aiding Adolf Hitler in his rise to power. The conditions identified are as follows:

- economic factors
- weakness of the existing political system
- social division
- impact of war.

Methods refer to the techniques used by a leader and political party to gain power. These techniques are the direct and controllable factors that suggest that they were actively involved in the establishment of their state. For example, Mao Zedong's ideological position was important to his popular appeal. The methods identified are as follows:

- role of leaders
- ideology
- force
- persuasion and coercion
- propaganda.

It is important to note that depending on the authoritarian or single-party state that you are studying, these factors will have differing levels of significance. When writing your essay you should be able to develop an argument that considers how certain conditions and methods contributed to the emergence of authoritarian states.

■ Methods for the consolidation and maintenance of power

Questions in this section are concerned with the methods used for power to be consolidated and then maintained throughout the authoritarian leader's rule. Consolidation refers to the immediate steps to secure power, so this might include securing borders, removing opposition groups and setting up political structures for the running of the state. Maintenance of power is a term we can use when looking at the methods used to keep the authority of the state throughout the regime's rule. The methods identified for the consolidation and maintenance of power are as follows:

- legal methods
- force
- charismatic leadership
- propaganda
- success and failure of foreign policy
- extent and treatment of opposition.

■ Aims and results of domestic policies

The final section is an exploration of domestic policy through the lens of social, economic, political and cultural policies. It is important to note that some of the policies can be used as evidence for the section on consolidation and maintenance of power. For example, Stalin's Five-Year Plans are an example of a domestic policy but also a method for controlling the USSR. This section also has a specific focus on the status and treatment of women and minority groups within the state. Finally, you should also consider the extent to which authoritarian control had been achieved.

UNDERSTANDING TERMINOLOGY

Here is a quick activity to reflect on your understanding of the different sections that you might write about on authoritarian states. Simply match up the terms to their definitions.

Term	Definition
Charismatic leadership	Methods used to secure power once an authoritarian state has been created
Consolidation	Often political measures to establish and maintain power through the use of laws. These could include writing constitutions
Foreign policy	Refers to discontent or inequality in society
Ideology	A set of guiding ideas that are used by individuals and political parties. This includes fascism
Legal methods	Policy measures outside a state including alliances, trade deals and military engagements
Minorities	Method used to ensure conformity to the rule of a leader. This often involves the development of a cult of personality
Social division	Groups in societies that are not dominant. They may experience repression or more inequality under specific authoritarian states. For example, religious groups and different ethnic groups

HISTORICAL CONCEPTS

A useful tool for understanding the case studies on authoritarian states is the use of historical concepts. If you can get into the habit of thinking about historical concepts when you engage with the content, it will help you to develop your ideas and analytical skills. Concepts are referred to in the rubric for the Paper 2 essays, so you should definitely engage with them in your writing. The concepts are listed below: have a go at writing what you understand about these concepts in relation to the study of History. Below are some notes on the concepts which you could have a look at when you have completed the activity.

Historical concepts:

- change
- continuity
- perspectives
- causality
- consequence
- significance.

> **Change** A broad concept within history, this concept is used regularly. When thinking about change, you could consider the types of change that might occur within an authoritarian state as a result of policies. Examples include social, economic or political change. When evaluating, think about whether the implemented change was successful or not.
>
> **Continuity** An underused, but useful concept. For this concept we can consider the lack of change. What stayed the same despite a governmental system trying to bring about a new direction in policy? For example, attitudes towards gender could be explored through this concept.
>
> **Perspectives** An essential part of historical investigation is to consider what perspectives might exist on a certain situation or event. An example could be looking at the importance of existing conditions versus methods used for the rise to power of an authoritarian state. Perspectives can also include the views of different agents in the process of history, including historians, people from the time and your own interpretations.
>
> **Causality** Causality is the bread and butter of analytical writing. This refers to developing an understanding of the reasons why something happened. Can you consider the reasons why a leader introduced specific economic policies? What were their motivations? Causality is thinking about why something happened or changed.
>
> **Consequence** This concept explores the effects of something that has taken place. In authoritarian states this might be the consequences of propaganda or the treatment of opposition parties. What were the effects? Consequence can also be categorized in different ways, such as short-term and long-term effects or cultural and social consequences.
>
> **Significance** We use significance when considering importance and it is very useful for developing historical arguments. For example, when considering foreign policy, what was the significance of these policies towards the maintenance of power? Could it be compared to other factors that may have had more or less impact?

The USSR under Joseph Stalin, 1924–53

On 5 March 1953 **Joseph Stalin** died. He had succeeded **Vladimir Lenin** as the leader of the USSR in the 1920s and introduced far-reaching policies that transformed the economic and social landscape of the country. Stalin dealt with any opposition, perceived or real, ferociously and introduced policies that impacted people across the USSR.

The establishment of the Soviet Union and Stalin's rise to power

Revised

When analysing the rule of Stalin, a consideration of Lenin's impact on the establishment of the USSR is also required. This is because the USSR as an authoritarian state came into existence under the rule of Lenin. In this section we will examine the conditions leading to the **Bolshevik Revolution** in 1917 as well as the conditions of the Soviet Union in its early years of creation under Lenin.

Conditions in which the Soviet Union emerged

The Soviet Union emerged due to a variety of circumstances including the social conditions facing people in the Russian Empire through to the impact of war and revolution.

Social division

- Prior to the Bolshevik Revolution, Russia was a large empire made up of many nationalities ruled by Tsar **Nicholas II**. Many of the nationalities within the Russian Empire sought independence.
- **Russification** was a policy introduced to suppress local languages and customs so that the dominant language and culture of the empire was Russian.
- The majority of people were agricultural labourers who lived in rural areas, most of whom existed in poverty. Agricultural labourers had gained more freedom after the **Emancipation of the Serfs** in 1861 but conditions continued to be difficult.
- Some industrialization had taken place in Russia, such as the development of the **Trans-Siberian Railway**. Working conditions for industrial workers were harsh, with long hours and poor living standards. Workers tended to labour in factories, in mines and on the railways.
- Protests against tsarist rule were frequent. The **1905 Revolution** was a serious challenge but was overcome by Nicholas II. He had to introduce political reforms in response to the protests, including creating a representative assembly, the **Duma**.
- A range of political groups was founded and developed in the early twentieth century, reflecting different perspectives on how the empire should be governed. These included the Bolsheviks, **Mensheviks**, **Kadets**, **Octobrists** and **Socialist Revolutionaries**.
- Tsarist rule ended with the **February Revolution** of 1917, which began as a series of protests against food shortages in the city of Petrograd (Saint Petersburg). After a few days of fighting in the city, the military joined the protesters and Tsar Nicholas II abdicated. This has sometimes been described as a 'revolution from below', reflecting the importance of social division in Russia at the time.

The establishment of the Soviet Union and Stalin's rise to power

REFLECTING ON LONG-TERM CAUSES

When writing about the establishment of the Soviet Union as an authoritarian state there is scope to discuss long-term causes to provide background and context to the conditions that made revolution more likely.

Complete the following table to reflect on the relative importance of the following long-term causes.

Long-term cause	Your explanation of its importance to the establishment of the Soviet Union
Social division, for example the conditions facing agricultural labourers and industrial workers in the early twentieth century	
Weakness of political system, for example the problems with the tsarist regime and the *Duma*, the unpopularity of Nicholas II	
Ideological challenges to tsarism, for example the growth of political groups and opposition (Liberals, Mensheviks, Bolsheviks), the influence of Karl Marx and Friedrich Engels	

SOURCE INVESTIGATION

Answer the questions below in relation to the sources.

SOURCE 1

Extract from Karl Marx and Friedrich Engels, *Manifesto of the Communist Party*, New York Labor News Co., New York, 1908. This book was first published in 1848.

The history of all hitherto existing society is the history of class struggles.

Freeman and slave, patrician and plebian, lord and serf, guildmaster and journeyman, in a word, oppressor and oppressed, stood in constant opposition to one another, carried on an uninterrupted, now hidden, now open fight, a fight that each time ended, either in a revolutionary reconstitution of society at large, or in the common ruin of the contending classes.

In the earlier epochs of history we find almost everywhere a complicated arrangement of society into various orders, a manifold gradation of social rank. In ancient Rome we have patricians, knights, plebeians, slaves; in the middle ages, feudal lords, vassals, guild masters, journeymen, apprentices, serfs; in almost all of these classes, again, subordinate gradations.

The modern bourgeois society that has sprouted from the ruins of feudal society has not done away with class antagonisms. It has but established new classes, new conditions of oppression, new forms of struggle in place of the old ones.

1. What do you think is meant by the parts of the source that have been underlined?
2. For what reasons would the ideas of Marx and Engels resonate with people living under the Russian Empire?

SOURCE 2

Extract from a letter to Nicholas II of January 1917 from Grand Duke Alexander Mikhailovich, quoted in P.D. Allan, *Russia and Eastern Europe*, Hodder Arnold, Sevenoaks, 1983, page 1.

The unrest grows; even the monarchist principle is beginning to totter; and those who defend the idea that Russia cannot exist without a Tsar lose the ground under their feet, since the facts of disorganization and lawlessness are manifest. A situation like this cannot last long. I repeat once more – it is impossible to rule the country without paying attention to the voice of the people, without meeting their needs, without a willingness to admit that the people themselves understand their own needs.

3. According to Source 2, what role did social division play in the February Revolution?

2 The USSR under Joseph Stalin, 1924–53

■ The impact of war
- Russia's involvement in the First World War was an important factor leading to the February Revolution in 1917. The war lowered people's morale and led to a loss of life, and there were severe food shortages.
- For example, at the **Battle of Tannenburg** over a few days in August 1914, close to 100,000 Russian soldiers were either killed or wounded. The leadership of Tsar Nicholas II during the war was heavily criticized as he took personal responsibility for the military command.
- The Bolsheviks promised 'peace, bread and land', a popular slogan in relation to the unpopularity of Russia's continued involvement in the First World War. The Bolsheviks' position against the war helped them to gain popularity to launch the October Revolution.
- In March 1918, the new Bolshevik government signed the **Treaty of Brest-Litovsk** which took Russia out of the war. It had harsh terms and was very unpopular.
- After the Bolsheviks took power they had to defend their position in the **Russian Civil War**.
- The Russian Civil War from 1917 to 1922 was largely a war between the Reds (Bolsheviks and the Red Army) and the Whites (different anti-Bolshevik groups) who also received support from other countries including Britain and Japan. There were also the Greens, who were peasant armies who fought to protect their own local interests.
- The Reds were able to overcome the Whites and win the war. This allowed them to consolidate their control. **Leon Trotsky**'s leadership of the Red Army played a key role in winning the war.

■ Economic conditions
- The poor economic situation facing the Russians was an important contributory factor to the revolutions in 1917. For example, there was worker discontent over low wages and poor conditions. There was also rising inflation during the First World War which increased prices of goods.
- During the Russian Civil War, Lenin introduced the economic policy called **War Communism**. This was a harsh series of policies intended to help the Bolsheviks win the civil war. It included rationing of food and goods, outlawing strikes, nationalizing industries and the requisition of crops from agricultural workers for centralized redistribution.
- War Communism was very unpopular with agricultural labourers and there was mass resistance. It also did not yield the results that were hoped for and production declined. The problems of War Communism were a major cause of the **Kronstadt Rebellion**.
- Subsequently, Lenin introduced the **New Economic Policy (NEP)** in 1921 as a way to address these problems. It was seen to be necessary to help the USSR recover from the impact of the civil war.
- The NEP ended the requisition of grain, allowed small levels of profit-making and enterprise, and somewhat relaxed the state control over the economy.
- Disagreement over economic policy was an important division within the **Bolshevik Party** that shaped the power struggle after Lenin's death.

■ Weakness of political system
- The Bolsheviks took power in October 1917, overthrowing the **Provisional Government**, which had been set up after the February Revolution as a temporary government.
- A new government structure was set up: a one-party, authoritarian state under the control of the **Communist Party of the Soviet Union (CPSU)**. The **Council of People's Commissars** and the **Secretariat** were set up under Lenin.
- The USSR was founded in 1922 after the end of the civil war.
- The new state was strongly authoritarian. Lenin made use of secret police, the *Cheka*, to deal with opposition, and religious groups were heavily repressed. Lenin made use of **purges** and **show trials**.
- **Factionalism** was banned within the CPSU. This meant that there was to be no open, free speech or criticism.
- Lenin was a believer in **democratic centralism**, which ensured that there was obedience towards the authority of the Soviet leadership. It was thought that the leadership was best placed to make the right decisions.

The establishment of the Soviet Union and Stalin's rise to power

TRAFFIC LIGHTS

How important do you think the following were to the establishment of the Soviet Union? Use the following code: red = not important, amber = slightly important and green = important.

Factor	Red, amber or green?	Explanation
High levels of poverty among the peasantry in the Russian countryside		
Russification: spreading Russian language and culture under Tsar Nicholas II		
Tsar Nicholas II's command of the army during the First World War		
The success of the October Revolution		
The political systems and structure set up by Lenin		
Ideology (Marxism and Lenin's adaptations)		
Russian Civil War		

WRITING PRACTICE: THE IMPORTANCE OF WAR

- Practise writing a paragraph that focuses on the importance of war for the establishment of the Soviet Union.
- Discuss the importance of the First World War and the Russian Civil War.
- You can use this template to help you to structure your writing.

> War was an important factor that led to the establishment of the USSR. The First World War had a major impact on the Russian Empire _____
>
> _____
>
> Furthermore, the Russian Civil War _____
>
> _____
>
> However, an alternative view is that _____
>
> _____

ESSAY WRITING HELP

Connectives are very useful for providing structure to history essays. Try to think of examples for the following types of connectives.

Contrasting	Alternatively, however
Comparing	
Emphasizing	
Adding	
Sequencing	
Providing examples	

- Reflect on how you might make better use of connectives in your writing.
- Think about how they can help you to bring out historical concepts (for example change, perspective) in your writing.

Methods for the establishment of the Soviet Union under Lenin and Stalin

As we have seen earlier, the Soviet Union emerged from the success of the Bolshevik Revolution and the victory of the Russian Civil War. This section will look at the methods used by Lenin in the early establishment of the Soviet Union as well as some of the factors that aided Stalin in his bid to take power after Lenin's death in 1924.

Ideology

Importance of Lenin

- Lenin had a profound impact on the ideological development of Marxism. He was also a major critic of imperialism, describing it as the 'highest stage of capitalism'.
- Following Marxist theory, Lenin proposed the 'dictatorship of the proletariat' as a means of creating the conditions for the establishment of a socialist state. Lenin proposed that a **vanguard party** should take the lead in this process.
- Lenin's **April Theses** of 1917 were part of an important ideological speech that laid out his priorities for the revolution and establishment of a new state.
- Once in power, Lenin's policies reflected his ideological position, for example land reform and setting up of authoritarian measures such as the secret police.
- Lenin showed flexibility with his ideology with the introduction of the NEP due to the problems created by the Russian Civil War and War Communism.

Importance of Stalin

- Stalin also played a key role in the ideological development of the Soviet Union. He declared himself a Marxist–Leninist and wanted to be viewed as a dedicated follower of Lenin.
- Stalin's policy of **Socialism in One Country** was a call to consolidate and modernize the Soviet Union rather than concern itself with spreading revolution worldwide.
- This position was popular as it promoted stability. It also differed from Leon Trotsky's position of **Permanent Revolution**, which advocated the need for continuous efforts to promote revolution overseas.

Role of leaders

A variety of leaders played important roles in the establishment of the Soviet Union. This section will consider the significance of Lenin, Trotsky and Stalin. You might also want to consider the roles of **Bukharin**, **Zinoviev** and **Kamenev**.

Lenin

- As mentioned above, Lenin was a political theorist whose writings and policies guided the Soviet Union.
- He provided leadership in the setting up of the political structures of the state, Russian Civil War, economic policy and social policies.

Trotsky

- Trotsky played both an important ideological role (formerly a Menshevik) and a practical role. He was one of the main organizers of the October Revolution. He wrote extensively on Marxist theory.
- He was commissar for foreign affairs initially and signed the unpopular Treaty of Brest-Litovsk.
- He led the Red Army successfully during the Russian Civil War. This was crucial to the survival of the Soviet Union.
- He was unable to take power after Lenin's death due to a combination of factors. One reason was his unwillingness to get involved in political infighting to secure his position.

Stalin

- Stalin wielded political influence due to the positions he held in the party from 1917 onwards. He worked as commissar for nationalities and was former editor of **Pravda**.
- Of particular note was his position as general secretary from 1922, which allowed him to have a clear awareness of the workings of the entire administration.
- He was viewed as a bureaucratic administrator by other members of the party. Nicknames include the 'grey blur' and 'comrade filing card'.

The establishment of the Soviet Union and Stalin's rise to power

- He had the power of **patronage**, which meant he could appoint his supporters into the party.
- When Lenin died in 1924, Stalin was able to position himself as successor in a variety of ways. These included organizing Lenin's funeral and presenting himself as a committed Leninist. He was fortunate that **Lenin's Testament** was never released as it was very critical of Stalin.

SOURCE INVESTIGATION

Answer the questions below with reference to the sources.

SOURCE 3

An extract from Lenin's 1902 pamphlet, 'What is to be done?', quoted in Anthony Wood, *The Russian Revolution*, second edition, Routledge, London, 1986, page 77.

An organization of workers must be first a trade organization; secondly, it must be as broad as possible; thirdly, it must be as little secret as possible … . An organization of revolutionaries, on the contrary, must embrace primarily and chiefly people whose profession consists of revolutionary activity. …

… In an autocratic country, the more we *narrow* the membership of such an organization, restricting it only to those who are professionally engaged in revolutionary activities and have received a professional training in the art of struggle against the political police, the more difficult will it be to 'catch' such an organization … .

4   What does Source 3 tell you about Lenin's views on the role of revolutionary groups?

_____

_____

SOURCE 4

An extract from Leon Trotsky, *The Permanent Revolution & Results and Prospects*, Red Letter Press, Seattle, 2010, page 313. Trotsky's book was first published in 1931.

The completion of the socialist revolution within national limits is unthinkable. … The socialist revolution begins on the national arena, it unfolds on the international arena, and is completed on the world arena.

5   How does the extract in Source 4 help you to understand Trotsky's ideological position?

_____

_____

STALIN, TROTSKY OR LENIN?

- Read through the statements below and decide whether they refer to Stalin, Trotsky or Lenin.
- Also write a comment on the significance of the factor.

Example	Lenin?	Stalin?	Trotsky?	Significance?
Proposed Socialism in One Country as an ideological position on revolution				
Made the decision to introduce the NEP after the Russian Civil War				
Proposed the need for a vanguard party to lead the revolution and build a socialist state				
Played a crucial role in both the October Revolution and the Russian Civil War				
Held positions of power that allowed him to place supporters into the party				
Was against both the NEP and Socialism in One Country				

The use of force

- Force played a role in the establishment of the Soviet Union; the **Red Terror** during the civil war years was a brutal repression and killing of supporters of the tsarist system.
- Lenin's secret police, the *Cheka*, carried out much of the terror, using extreme methods of torture and execution.
- Concentration camps were set up for those opposing the regime and there were also purges and show trials, such as the **1922 Moscow Trial of the Socialist Revolutionaries**.
- Any opposition, for instance peasant resistance in the countryside, was dealt with harshly.
- Religious groups were repressed under Lenin. Many Church leaders were arrested or killed.

Persuasion and coercion

- Persuasion and coercion played an important role in Stalin's acquisition of power after the death of Lenin.
- He was able to fill the party with his supporters due to his position as general secretary from 1922 onwards. Previously, he had also held positions of people's commissar for nationalities, liaison officer between the **Politburo** and **Orgburo**, and head of the workers' and peasants inspectorate.
- Stalin positioned himself as Lenin's successor, delivering a speech at his funeral.
- Stalin successfully isolated and removed his opponents. He supported Kamenev and Zinoviev when they were in conflict with Trotsky. He then turned on all three of them in 1927, leading to their dismissal from the party.
- Stalin was able to time his opinions on certain policies such as the NEP in a way that was favourable to him, understanding the mood of the party.
- After the defeat of the left, Stalin worked to remove the right opposition of Bukharin, **Tomsky** and **Rykov** as a means of introducing the policies of **collectivization** and **industrialization**.

Propaganda

- *Pravda* became the official newspaper of the CPSU. It was used to promote the party's achievements and ideology.
- The October Revolution was regularly glorified in propaganda, as was the role of Lenin. A cult of personality developed around Lenin.
- Bolshevik propaganda was used during the civil war to help with the war effort, for instance the use of posters and **agitprop** trains that had revolutionary images to support the Reds.
- Censorship was widespread in literature and the arts to remove anti-Bolshevik ideas.

The establishment of the Soviet Union and Stalin's rise to power

SUMMARY NOTES

Create a revision table summarizing the factors that led to the establishment of the Soviet Union under Lenin and Stalin. Use the framework provided below.

Factor	Explanation and examples
Economic conditions	
Weakness of political system	
Social division	
Impact of war	
Role of leaders	
Ideology	
Persuasion and coercion	
Propaganda	
Force	

CHRONOLOGY ACTIVITY

The following events are all relevant to Stalin's rise to power after Lenin's death:

- Lenin's Testament not being read out to the members of the CPSU.
- Stalin's backing away from the NEP and launching an attack on Bukharin and the right wing of the party.
- The formation of the united opposition of Trotsky, Kamenev and Zinoviev against Stalin and the right wing of the party.
- Stalin was seen as the clear frontrunner for the Soviet leadership.
- Trotsky criticized Kamenev and Zinoviev in his **Lessons of October**.
- Expulsion of Trotsky, Kamenev and Zinoviev from the party after accusations of factionalism.

Check your understanding of the events leading to Stalin's rise to power by going through the sequence and placing them in the correct order.

Year	Event
1924 (May)	
1924 (October)	
1926	
1927	
1928	
1929	

FURTHER PRACTICE QUESTIONS

The following questions can also help you to revise the establishment of the Soviet Union and the rise to power of Stalin.

- Examine the importance of persuasion and coercion in the rise to power of one authoritarian ruler.
- 'Socially divided societies provide the ideal conditions for the establishment of authoritarian states.' To what extent do you agree with this statement? Refer to two different authoritarian states in your answer.

2 The USSR under Joseph Stalin, 1924–53

Stalin's consolidation and maintenance of power

Revised

By 1929, Stalin had emerged as the sole leader of the Soviet Union. He had successfully removed any challenges to his bid for power from both the left and right wings of the CPSU. In the years following, he introduced policies to consolidate and maintain his control over the Soviet Union.

Methods for the consolidation and maintenance of power

Legal methods: political

- Politically, the structures of the Soviet Union had been established before Stalin took power.
- These included the status of the CPSU and the outlawing of any other political parties, as well as the organization of the party and legislative apparatus.
- One major political change that Stalin introduced was the 1936 constitution.
- The constitution provided for democratic participation of men and women over the age of eighteen. However, in elections they were only able to vote for candidates approved by the party.
- Article 125 of the constitution stated that citizens of the USSR had the freedom of speech, a free press and the right of assembly. However, as seen by the treatment of opposition, and by the use of authoritarian policies, these freedoms never really materialized.

Legal methods: economic

- Stalin wanted to transform the Soviet Union; this fitted with his policy of Socialism in One Country. He wanted the USSR to catch up with the developed nations of the West.
- Stalin proposed to do this through mass industrialization and collectivization by way of a series of Five-Year Plans. Part of the motivation for this was to move away from the NEP.

Collectivization

- Large areas of land were to be farmed collectively under this process. One type of collective farm, the *kolkhoz*, would comprise between 50 and 100 households.
- Collectivization meant that the state took control of the land and agricultural labourers then farmed it. The state took centralized control of grain production and distribution.
- Stalin identified the *kulaks* as a group who needed to be removed as a class. The *kulaks* were a group of richer agricultural labourers who had benefited under the NEP. Among other things, they were accused of hoarding grain.
- De-kulakization, therefore, was a policy that accompanied collectivization. Many people were attacked violently or killed in this process. There were also mass deportations of *kulaks* during the early 1930s.
- The collectivization process was successful in its intention of bringing peasant farms under state control. By the early 1940s, the process had led to the collectivization of almost all of the Soviet Union's farmland.
- There was significant resistance to collectivization from agricultural labourers, who felt that their lifestyles were threatened. Resistance came in many forms, both peaceful and violent, but grew increasingly violent through actions such as arson attacks.
- The consequences of collectivization were devastating for agricultural labourers. Their way of life had been completely transformed; there was mass starvation in the 1930s. Millions died in the famines in Ukraine and Kazakhstan, seen as a direct result of the upheaval in the countryside.
- Many agricultural labourers left the countryside to work in the mass industrialization projects being established.

Industrialization

- Stalin carried out several Five-Year Plans while he was leader of the Soviet Union.
- The Five-Year Plans involved a series of targets for industrial production.
- The first Five-Year Plan saw a significant increase in the production of coal and iron.
- Industrial areas expanded rapidly to try and reach these targets. The development of the city of Magnitogorsk for steel production is one such example.
- Major industrial projects were completed during the first Five-Year Plan, including the White Sea–Baltic Canal and the Dnieprostroi Dam. Forced labour often was used to carry out these projects.
- Workers were encouraged and given incentives to work as hard as possible on these projects. Aleksei Stakhanov was used as a role model as he had managed to extract 102 tonnes of coal in six hours, a record amount. This created unrealistic expectations for workers.

- Industrialization continued through the Five-Year Plans prior to the Second World War. There was a great deal of evidence that these were successful in developing the Soviet Union's industrial base and increasing production.
- The major problem of both industrialization and collectivization was the human cost. Living conditions were very difficult for workers throughout the Soviet Union. Safety was very poor for industrial workers and hours were long. The famines in the countryside are further evidence of the human cost of these policies.

THE IMPACT OF INDUSTRIALIZATION

Consider Sources 5–7 below. How can you use them to explain the following?

- The success and failure of Stalin's economic policies.
- The importance of economic policies towards Stalin's consolidation and maintenance of power.

SOURCE 5

Industrial output during the first three Five-Year Plans, quoted in Michael Lynch, *Bolshevik and Stalinist Russia: 1917–64*, Hodder Education, London, 2015, page 102.

Product	1927	1930	1932	1935	1937	1940
Coal (millions of tonnes)	35	60	64	100	128	150
Steel (millions of tonnes)	3	5	6	13	18	18
Oil (millions of tonnes)	12	17	21	24	26	26
Electricity (millions of kWh)	18	22	20	45	80	90

SOURCE 6

Extract from David Evans and Jane Jenkins, *Years of Russia, the USSR and the Collapse of Soviet Communism*, Hodder Education, London, 2008, pages 288 and 289. Gosplan was the name for the Soviet state planning committee.

Soviet claims and statistics relating to the Five-Year Plan lost credibility because they were influenced by the needs of propaganda and by the inflated returns provided by Gosplan. Yet, even though we know that the Plans often failed to reach their targets and were affected by confusion, waste and inefficiency, there is no doubt that Stalin's industrialization of the Soviet Union was a remarkable achievement … Stalin had changed the face of the Soviet Union. It was now a country of factories, iron and steel works, hydro-electric dams and much improved systems of transport and communication … On the other hand it might be argued that millions had died and the people forced to endure hard labour, shortages, reduced living standards and the loss of their personal liberties in order to create a better life for future generations of Russians.

SOURCE 7

Blast furnace built during the first Five-Year Plan at Magnitogorsk by a combination of 'shock workers' and forced labour.

Force and the treatment of opposition

- Stalin made full use of purges to remove any opposition to his authority.
- An early Stalinist purge was the **Ryutin Affair** in 1932. Ryutin had written in opposition to Stalin, describing him as the 'gravedigger of the revolution' and calling for a halt to the economic policy of collectivization. He and his supporters had tried to organize resistance but were caught, put on trial and expelled from the party. Ryutin was later executed in 1937.
- Stalin used a range of methods to enforce control, including the increased use of the secret police: the **NKVD** (People's Commissariat for Internal Affairs).
- Numerous labour camps were set up across the Soviet Union. These *gulags* were holding facilities for any opposition figures and prisoners under Stalin.
- The murder of **Sergei Kirov** was a turning point in the mid-1930s. Kirov was a popular member of the CPSU and was potentially someone who could have launched a successful bid to oust Stalin from power. His death was beneficial to Stalin as it took away this challenge. There are suggestions that Stalin may have arranged his death.
- After the murder, a series of moves by Stalin intensified the purges and increased his power over the party. This included the arrest, imprisonment, execution and exile of thousands of party members. Stalin was then able to appoint his most loyal supporters in important positions of power.
- Many members of the party did not oppose these purges as they were loyal to Stalin and wanted to advance their own careers.

The Great Terror

- The purges intensified in the late 1930s. This time has become known as the **Great Terror**.
- Various show trials were held during this time. The trial of Kamenev and Zinoviev in 1936 saw Stalin removing old rivals on the left of the party. In 1938, the trials of Bukharin, Rykov and Tomsky saw him take on the right of the party. The public nature of these trials had a strong impact on Stalin's control over the Soviet Union.
- The military was heavily purged in 1937, with officers especially targeted.
- The Great Terror also affected people across different sectors of society. An atmosphere of fear was created, with the secret police carrying out many mass killings and with millions sent to work in the *gulags*.
- The purges continued during the Second World War and into Stalin's final years in power, such as the **Doctors' Plot** in the early 1950s.

Charismatic leadership and the dissemination of propaganda

- Propaganda was used to promote Stalin's authority and his policies. A cult of personality was created.
- He was often pictured next to Lenin to give him the clear position as the rightful successor.
- Trotsky's historical reputation was weakened and he was sometimes removed from photographs along with other prominent Bolsheviks from early Soviet history.
- Artistic styles heavily promoted **socialist realism**, which could be understood by the public and would promote the values and policies of the party.
- Stalin described writers as 'engineers of the human soul', seeing them as significant to shaping the thoughts and culture of the Soviet Union. Such propaganda books included *How the Steel was Tempered* from 1932 and *The Great Conveyor Belt* of 1934.
- Censorship was enforced. For example, many influential writers, film-makers and artists were curtailed under Stalin if they were seen as too liberal or too encouraging of free speech.
- Propaganda was everywhere, including architecture, sculpture, film, music and literature.
- The cult of personality around Stalin evolved after the success of the Second World War. He was often pictured wearing white clothes and viewed as the saviour of the people.

Stalin's consolidation and maintenance of power

MIND MAP ON STALIN'S USE OF FORCE AND TERROR

Force and terror played an important role in Stalin's consolidation and maintenance of power. There were a wide range of purges and measures that were used to control the party and more broadly the people of the USSR. Create a mind map to show the different ways that Stalin used force once in power. You can use Sources 8 and 9 to help develop the details on your mind map and the template below as a design for this task.

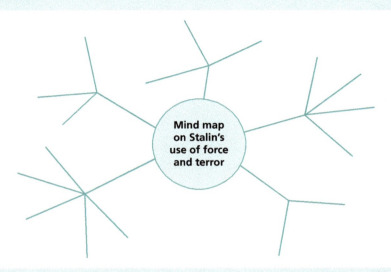

SOURCE 8

A map showing the location of *gulags* in the USSR.

SOURCE 9

Extract from Jacques Rossi, *The Gulag Handbook: An Historical Dictionary of Soviet Penitentiary Institutions and Terms Related to the Forced Labor Camps*, Office of the Secretary of Defense, Washington, DC, 1985. This extract describes the conditions in a *gulag*.

During their non-working hours, prisoners typically lived in a camp zone surrounded by a fence or barbed wire, overlooked by armed guards in watch towers. The zone contained a number of overcrowded, stinking, poorly-heated barracks. Life in a camp zone was brutal and violent. Prisoners competed for access to all of life's necessities, and violence among the prisoners was commonplace. If they survived hunger, disease, the harsh elements, heavy labor, and their fellow prisoners, they might succumb to arbitrary violence at the hands of camp guards. All the while, prisoners were watched by informers – fellow prisoners always looking for some misstep to report to Gulag authorities.

Stalin's foreign policies

Early foreign policy
- After the upheaval of the Russian Civil War, early Soviet policy focused on recovery from the war and building peace. As the only communist state in the world, the USSR was quite isolated.
- The USSR was able to make treaties with Germany during the 1920s and received diplomatic recognition from Britain and France.
- **Comintern** had been set up to aid communist parties around the world. It was very active in the 1920s, as seen by its involvement in China. Comintern took on a more radical approach in Germany and encouraged the communists to challenge the Social Democrats, effectively causing unrest to an important opposition group to the Nazis.
- As Stalin consolidated his power, he wanted to reduce the role of Comintern as well as focus more on domestic concerns. His policy of Socialism in One Country was a reflection of this.

Foreign policy before the Second World War
- Relations between the Soviet Union and Germany grew tense after the rise to power of Hitler in 1933. Stalin realized that he needed to build alliances in Europe. Despite this, the USSR still signed a trade deal with Germany in 1934.
- In September 1934, Stalin was able to secure the Soviet Union's membership of the League of Nations. This was part of a wider move towards **collective security** at the time. Stalin was also able to make diplomatic progress, with security pacts with both France and Czechoslovakia in 1935.
- The Soviet Union involved itself in the Spanish Civil War, reflecting its concerns about the growth of fascism in Europe. Furthermore, the **Anti-Comintern Pact** of 1936 between Germany and Japan was a clear signal to Stalin of the need for alliances.
- The **Munich Agreement** of 1938 was an accord between Britain, France and Germany that allowed Hitler to take over the Sudetenland in Czechoslovakia. The USSR was excluded from the negotiations. This was an example of appeasement that concerned Stalin and can be seen as a reason for his agreeing to the **Nazi–Soviet Pact** in 1939.
- An unexpected move during this time was the signing of the Nazi–Soviet Pact that sought to divide territorial interests in Eastern Europe between Germany and the USSR. Explanations for this move by Stalin can be apportioned to his lack of solid alliances in Europe as well as territorial and security interests. The signing of the Nazi–Soviet Pact brought Hitler and Stalin together for two years, during which time Stalin was able to regain lost territory from the Treaty of Brest-Litovsk and both countries divided Poland.
- Despite the signing of the pact, Hitler invaded the Soviet Union in 1941. Stalin was brought into the Second World War.

> **CONCEPT FOCUS: SIGNIFICANCE**
>
> One of the history concepts that can be used in your essays is significance. Within the study of History, this refers to explaining the relevant importance of an event or action. For this concept, consider the reasons why historians would place more emphasis on certain evidence, essentially viewing some pieces of evidence as more significant than others.

The Second World War and afterwards
- The Soviet Union's victory over Nazi Germany gave Stalin a huge popularity boost at home. Stalin's cult of personality expanded rapidly as a result of the war.
- The Soviet Union was severely affected by the war, with more than 20 million casualties.
- Stalin's international profile was transformed as a result of the war, as a member of the **Grand Alliance** and his role during the **Yalta Conference** and **Potsdam Conference**.
- Stalin sought to strengthen the position of the Soviet Union internationally after the war and was instrumental in the **Sovietization of Eastern Europe**. This process saw many Eastern European countries become communist and was a major source of tension between the Soviet Union and the USA.

FOREIGN POLICY ESSAY PLAN

Discuss the ways that foreign policy contributes to the maintenance of power for authoritarian states. Refer to two authoritarian states from different regions in your response.

Create an essay plan for the question above. Think about the main points you will include and remember to explain the significance of the examples provided:

- This essay question is asking you to explore foreign policy in two different authoritarian states.
- When you have a question like this it is essential that you write about leaders from different regions.
- As both Stalin and Hitler are from the same region, you would not be allowed to write about these two leaders in this response.
- However, it would be acceptable to write about Stalin and Mao (or indeed Castro and Perón) in the response.

ELIMINATE IRRELEVANCE

Read through the following paragraph from a student answer to the above essay question. Cross out any sections of the paragraph that seem irrelevant and not focused on the question requirements.

> Foreign policy plays a crucial role in the maintenance of power for authoritarian states. Even in the twenty-first century we can see that successful foreign policies can have a positive impact on how different countries fare. Stalin's foreign policy had different priorities at different stages of his leadership over the USSR. Early on, with the policies of industrialization and collectivization, Stalin prioritized domestic development rather than an expansionist foreign policy. Factories were built across the Soviet Union and a major focus was on the development of heavy industry. However, as fascism became increasing popular across Europe, Stalin increasingly realized the need for collective security and sought stronger alliances.

Stalin's domestic policies: aims and results

As well as the massive changes brought about by industrialization, collectivization and the purges, a variety of social and cultural policies sought to remould Soviet society in line with Stalin's ideological principles.

Cultural policies

Literature
- Stalin sought to impose strict controls on writers in the Soviet Union.
- He once described writers as the 'engineers of the human soul', reflecting his feeling that they can have a transformative effect on the lives of people.
- Socialist realism was promoted in literature. Works needed to be easily understandable to the masses and to promote suitable role models.
- A famous work from the era was *How the Steel was Tempered* by **Nikolai Ostrovsky**.
- Close control and censorship prevented free speech in writing. Many writers were persecuted under Stalin's regime, including **Aleksandr Solzhenitsyn**, who later wrote *The Gulag Archipelago*.

Theatre and film
- Film production was strictly controlled under Stalin. During the Five-Year Plans, films that promoted industrialization were encouraged. During the purges and Great Terror a large number of films were censored.
- A similar situation is seen in theatre. A notable theatre director at the time, **Vsevolod Meyerhold**, opposed socialist realism. Despite being a high-profile name in theatre, he was arrested in 1938 and executed.

Painting, sculpture and music
- There were two main aims of painting and sculpture: to promote socialist realism and to strengthen the authority of Stalin.
- A famous sculpture was *Worker and Kolkhoz Woman*, made in 1937 by **Vera Mukhina**.
- Images of the family were discouraged in painting and the emphasis on the collective and work was prioritized.
- Stalin also promoted socialist realism in music, preferring a loud and positive-sounding melody, usually played in a major key. Once again, it was to be simplistic and able to have a mass appeal.

Stalin's domestic policies: aims and results

THE ROLE OF PROPAGANDA

Consider the following examples of propaganda and reflect on how they would contribute to Stalin's maintenance of power.

Example of propaganda	Explanation of significance
Poster showing Stalin steering a ship with the flag of the USSR in the background	
A painting showing a group of farm workers eating food together. The painting is called *A Collective Farm Feast*	
A photograph of Lenin addressing troops in 1920. Both Trotsky and Kamenev have been edited out of the picture	
A sculpture called *Worker and Kolkhoz Woman* (see Source 10)	
A book called *Energy* by Feodor Gladkov, published in 1932, that tells of the heroism of a group of construction workers	

SOURCE 10

A famous sculpture of 1937 called *Worker and Kolkhoz Woman* by Vera Mukhina, photographed in Moscow, 2016.

Social policies

Treatment of religion
- Religion was heavily repressed from the outset of the Soviet Union.
- The **Russian Orthodox Church** was the main religion targeted by the CPSU. There was resistance in the countryside, where religious traditions were more deep-rooted and held as sacred to people's lives.
- During the Great Terror the attacks on religion intensified. A large number of priests and religious figures were arrested. The vast majority of churches were closed down.
- Stalin's cult of personality worked to deify him as a god. Subsequently, a new type of religion could be observed in the Soviet Union. A similar state of affairs was seen in other authoritarian states in the twentieth century such as Mao's China and **Kim Il-Sung** in North Korea.
- Islam was also repressed and discouraged under Stalin, with mosques and religious schools closed down.
- The USSR also tried to ban Muslim women from wearing veils in a policy called *hujum*, seeing it as a restriction to gender equality. This policy largely failed.
- During the Second World War, attacks on religion lessened in an effort to get the whole of the Soviet Union behind the war effort. Religion was used to spread messages of nationalism and collective effort in the war.

Education under Stalin
- Education under Stalin was more traditional than the changes introduced by Lenin.
- School was compulsory until the age of fifteen.
- Government-regulated textbooks were used in classes, and there was an emphasis on testing and examinations.
- As well as learning about traditional subjects, students learned ideological theory and the teachings of **Karl Marx**.
- Some students continued after the age of fifteen; these were the students who would go on to take the elite positions in society.
- Outside school, campaigns trained illiterate adults how to read and write.
- The education system helped to grow a group known as the *nomenklatura*. Its members were the elite who ran the country. These were usually the children of party members who went on to higher education, reinforcing the power of this group.

Treatment of women
- As in education, Stalin was more conservative in social policy regarding women's rights than Lenin. This was known as the **Great Retreat**.
- Under Lenin, a variety of socially progressive laws had been introduced that sought to give women more rights over marriage, work and the family.
- Stalin looked to promote family values and also to discourage divorce and sexual freedom. He wanted a 'reconstruction of the family on a new socialist basis'.
- The **1936 Family Code** (the third family code since the revolution of 1917) made divorce more difficult; same-sex relationships were made illegal and abortion was discouraged.
- Trotsky strongly criticized the Great Retreat in his book *The Revolution Betrayed*.
- During the Second World War, an increase in birth rate was encouraged with a system of incentives and punishments. Women who had many children were celebrated, abortion was made illegal and taxes were higher for families with fewer children.
- The Great Retreat meant that the role of women's rights was placed behind the needs of the Soviet Union during both the Five-Year Plans and the Second World War. Many of the progressive changes that appeared in the early years of the Soviet Union were reversed.

Treatment of minority groups
- Stalin wanted to discourage nationalism and independence movements within the different Soviet republics.
- There were mass deportations of minority groups under Stalin, often to the more remote areas of Siberia or Kazakhstan. The people deported were typically from areas which Stalin saw as a threat to the unity of the Soviet Union. This was an example of **ethnic cleansing**.
- The scale of the deportations increased during the Second World War.

ESSAY PLAN

To what extent did Stalin achieve authoritarian control over the USSR?

Look at the essay question above. It asks you to consider the extent of Stalin's authoritarian control over the Soviet Union. In the table there are a range of factors. For each one, explain how this could be used within an answer to this question. Now create an essay plan for this question. How would you structure a response to this question? Is there scope to bring in perspectives? Historical comparison? Will you make reference to any of the history concepts? Reflect on how your response would change if you were writing about a different authoritarian state. What would be the significant similarities and differences?

Factor	How could this be used in your response?	What examples could you use to develop this point?
The development of a command economy with far-reaching industrial and agricultural policies		
The development of a cult of personality and the widespread use of propaganda		
Purging of political opposition, use of a secret police and prison camps		
Stalin's ideological position, including Socialism in One Country and democratic centralism		
The Great Retreat, social policies that sought to reinforce more traditional values in education and family life		

Exam focus

Sample question and answer

Have a look through this student answer to the essay question. Consider the strengths and limitations of the response.

Analyse the role of force and propaganda as methods for the consolidation and maintenance of power in one authoritarian state.

By the late 1920s, Joseph Stalin had emerged as the leader of the Soviet Union. He had succeeded to his position in the years following the death of Lenin using a variety of methods, including the isolation of his opponents in the CPSU. Once in power, he sought to both consolidate and maintain his position as leader of the USSR. Two important methods in doing so can be seen in the use of force and the dissemination of propaganda. Overall, it can be argued that Stalin stayed in power through strict authoritarian control that aimed to transform Soviet society. Force and propaganda were important techniques that allowed him to achieve these aims. • — *The student has provided a clear thesis statement which gives an indication of the line of argument.*

Force can be defined as measures involving highly authoritarian law and order, violence and fierce treatment of opposition. Within Stalin's rule we can find evidence of these measures. One of Stalin's major aims for the Soviet economy was collectivization and industrialization. In order to achieve this he identified the kulaks as a class enemy. The kulaks could be broadly described as the richer agricultural labourers who had benefited under the New Economic Policy of the 1920s. Once collectivization began, Stalin ordered a process of de-kulakization that involved mass deportations, arrests and killings. This carried a high human cost but in effect demonstrated the nature of Stalinist authority, contributing to his maintenance and consolidation of power. Evidence of success can be seen in the fact that the vast majority of Soviet land had been collectivized by 1939. • — *The student defines the terms.* / *Relevant example provided.*

Stalin's rule also included a wide range of purges of political opposition. A good example of this can be seen in the Ryutin Affair, where the policy of collectivization, as well as Stalin's leadership, was called into question by Ryutin in the early 1930s, when he published a 200-page criticism. Stalin's reaction essentially sought to silence the opposition. Ryutin and his supporters were arrested and expelled from the party. Ryutin was later executed. This was an early indication of how Stalin would deal with opposition within the party. Throughout the 1930s there were further purges of political opposition. • — *Relevance of the example is explained here.*

The extent of the purging of political opposition under the Stalinist regime can be seen in the Great Terror which began in 1936. Of particular note were the public show trials where CPSU members confessed to different crimes against the state. Old rivals Kamenev and Zinoviev were put on trial in 1937 and Bukharin in 1938. It is likely that those on trial were forced to confess to crimes. The purges affected both the left and right factions of the party. The military were also under scrutiny during this period. In sum, thousands of party members and military officers during this time were purged from their positions. Many of these people ended up in gulags, the prison camps that were distributed widely across the USSR in inhospitable locations with harsh conditions. • — *Good development point to elaborate further on the treatment of opposition and the use of force.*

Force, therefore, was a major factor in the Stalin administration. Interpretations vary on the extent of Stalin's involvement. Some historians have suggested that the Soviet Union was an example of a totalitarian state, a society under total control, with force and repression being major factors. The concept of totalitarianism was made popular by the political philosopher Hannah Arendt in her work 'The Origins of Totalitarianism'. This interpretation places emphasis on the role of terror and force in the maintenance of authoritarian states. However, more recent interpretations have suggested that the Soviet Union was not as strictly controlled as first perceived and that much of the violence carried out was haphazard and disorganized.

> It would have been worthwhile to provide an example of this.

Another method of control for the maintenance and consolidation of power was propaganda. Playing a major role in a variety of authoritarian states in the twentieth century, it was also a major feature of the USSR. Propaganda techniques can be viewed in a wide variety of forms including art, films, music, posters, newspapers and education. Accompanying propaganda was censorship, which sought to exclude certain views or distort perceptions.

Stalin had been attuned to the power of propaganda from his rise to power, where he made sure that he was viewed as the rightful successor to Lenin. He maintained this image once in power, with artworks that portrayed the two rulers together, or working together. He also diminished the role of his opponents through propaganda, for example removing Trotsky from historical photographs to diminish his significance to the party.

Propaganda often relied on the use of socialist realism, an artistic technique that emphasized realistic imagery of workers and farmers. This had two main aims: first, it was designed to be easily understood by large numbers of people within the USSR, and second, it served to support CPSU ideology, such as the policies of collectivization and industrialization.

> Good example to explain the aims of propaganda.

Education was an important area of social life where propaganda could be implemented. Of note is the more conservative approach of the Stalinist era, favouring traditional examinations and discipline in schools. This is in contrast to the more radical policies under Lenin, which placed a high value on removing hierarchies within the school system and introducing more practical subjects. Stalin, in what has been known as the 'Great Retreat', favoured stability; however, the 'benefits' of Marxist ideology were a major feature of education. Furthermore, the state controlled the textbooks and the curriculum, which subsequently worked as both a form of propaganda and censorship to encourage compliance with the regime.

> Contrast point showing historical awareness.

Overall, force and propaganda played an important role in Stalin's consolidation and maintenance of power and were major features of life in the USSR through the years of his rule. They helped him to control society, through both repression and thought control.

> The conclusion is clear and consistent with the essay.

> Clearly written with analysis and explanation of examples throughout. Some historical detail could have been developed further on some of the examples, for example socialist realism. There is good historical awareness and there are some points of comparison.

Exam practice

- What are your thoughts on this response?
- What strengths can you identify?
- How could the response be further developed?

Have a go at writing an answer to the question yourself or try out some other essay questions, such as those below.

1. Examine the importance of charismatic leadership towards the maintenance of power in two authoritarian states.

2. Evaluate the role of legal methods in the consolidation and maintenance of power in two authoritarian states.

3. Discuss the ways in which women and minority groups were affected by the rule of one authoritarian state.

Germany under Adolf Hitler, 1933–45

On 30 January 1933, **Adolf Hitler** was sworn into office by President **Paul von Hindenburg** as the chancellor of Germany. Hitler's rise to power was the result of a variety of factors that have been debated by historians ever since. Once in power, Hitler was able to consolidate control and went on to transform German society through domestic policies that aligned with the extreme views of his ideology, Nazism. Furthermore, Hitler went on to conduct a war against multiple nations that ultimately led to his own death and the defeat of the regime in 1945.

Hitler's rise to power

Revised

■ Conditions in which states emerged

Part of the reason to explain the rise of Hitler can be seen in the conditions facing Germany in the aftermath of the First World War up until the 1930s. It can be argued that these conditions favoured Hitler, allowing him to increase the electoral appeal of the Nazi Party and subsequently take control.

■ Impact of war

- Many Germans felt humiliated after the loss of the First World War. The war had been popularly embraced in 1914 and to lose after many years of fighting, accompanied by the severe loss of life, was received very badly throughout Germany.
- Furthermore, a great deal of resentment was created in 1918 with the creation of the **stab in the back myth** suggesting that the army had been betrayed by those who supported left-wing revolution at home and the people who had signed the armistice.
- The people who had signed the armistice became known as the **November Criminals**.
- People were further angered by the harsh terms of the **Treaty of Versailles** in 1919 that was agreed on during the Paris Peace Conference. It was described as a **diktat** or dictated peace; Germany had no say in the terms of the treaty or discussions.

> **SENSITIVE CONTENT:** You should note that some images and sources covered in this chapter include sensitive content which is potentially upsetting.

■ Outcomes of the Treaty of Versailles

The Treaty of Versailles dealt with Germany after the First World War and led to a variety of political and economic consequences for the country that included the following:

- **Reparations** to be paid in compensation for war damage.
- The acceptance of **Article 231** (see Source 2 opposite), a war guilt clause which meant that Germany had to take full responsibility for starting the war.
- There was a reduction of the German armed forces, with no submarines or air force, and the army was to be reduced to 100,000 men.
- German overseas colonies in Africa and Asia were confiscated.
- There was also a loss of territory in Europe, for example the region of Alsace-Lorraine was given to France.

■ Social division

The First World War had led to a widespread loss of life and left many people wounded. There was much anger and resentment. There was also an influenza pandemic in 1918 which severely affected Germany. This all contributed to a chaotic and divided society after the war:

- Immediately after the war there were numerous attempts to control Germany and different political ideas were being advocated. Encouraged by the success of the Bolsheviks in Russia, communist ideas were popular at this point. This was especially due to the wide differences in socio-economic status between the wealthy aristocracy and the poorer workers.
- The German revolution in the aftermath of the war demonstrated the increased popularity of socialist and communist ideologies. During the revolution, there was civil unrest and worker strikes, including the **Spartacist Uprising** in January 1919.
- The revolutionary period ended with the proclamation of the **Weimar Republic** in 1919.
- A range of political parties developed in Germany after the war and during the Weimar era, reflecting the range of opinions prevalent in the country. The table on page 32 summarizes some of the major parties.

Hitler's rise to power

SOURCE INVESTIGATION

Consider the sources and complete the accompanying questions.

SOURCE 1

An anti-Semitic cartoon produced in Austria shortly after the war illustrating the stab in the back myth.

1. What is the message of this political cartoon?

SOURCE 2

Selected articles from the Treaty of Versailles, quoted in The Avalon Project, Harvard Law School (available at http://avalon.law.yale.edu/imt/partiv.asp).

Article 119: Germany renounces in favour of the Principal Allied and Associated Powers all her rights and titles over her oversea possessions.

Article 159: The German military forces shall be demobilised and reduced as prescribed hereinafter.

Article 231: The Allied and Associated Governments affirm and Germany accepts the responsibility of Germany and her allies for causing all the loss and damage to which the Allied and Associated Governments and their nationals have been subjected as a consequence of the war imposed upon them by the aggression of Germany and her allies.

2. How do you think the Treaty of Versailles would have been received in Germany?

EXPLAIN THE SIGNIFICANCE

- Explain how the First World War would have affected Hitler's ideological position.
- Think about the significance of the factors mentioned in the speech bubbles.

- The stab in the back myth
- The Treaty of Versailles
- Anti-Semitism and anti-communist beliefs

3 Germany under Adolf Hitler, 1933–45

■ Political parties during the Weimar Era

Social Democratic Party (SPD)	The Social Democratic Party (SPD) was a socialist party that had been involved in the German revolution and establishment of the Weimar Republic. It was politically more moderate than other left-wing groups such as the Spartacists and communists. An important SPD member was Friedrich Ebert, who held the position of president of the Weimar Republic between 1918 and 1925
National Socialist German Workers' Party (NSDAP)	Originally the German Workers' Party (DAP) under the leadership of Anton Drexler. The National Socialist German Workers' Party (NSDAP) was formed in 1920 with Hitler as a prominent member. Hitler became leader of the party early on and its ideology of national socialism was characterized by anti-Semitism and nationalism
German People's Party (DVP)	The German People's Party (DVP) was formed at the end of the war. This party was a liberal–conservative party that enjoyed some success during the Weimar era. Its most famous politician was Gustav Stresemann, who was credited for many of the improvements in Germany in the late 1920s
Catholic Centre Party (Zentrum)	Drawing its support from Catholics and moderate Protestants, the Catholic Centre Party (Zentrum) was centrist but held opinions across the political spectrum. It was part of many of the governing coalitions of the Weimar era
Communist Party (KPD)	Formed from ex-members of the SPD and the Spartacists, the Communist Party (KPD) held support and influence through the 1920s and had an increase in electoral popularity during the depression. It was disbanded and forcibly repressed by the Nazis after they took power, with many members ending up in concentration camps

■ Weakness of political system

Following the abdication of Kaiser Wilhelm II after the war, the Weimar Republic was established in January 1919. In the following August the constitution was written:

- The republic's constitution was far more democratic than the previous political system.
- Every seven years a president was democratically elected who held emergency powers and control over the military. The president also appointed the chancellor.
- There was a democratically elected Reichstag, voted for by men and women over the age of twenty.

However, there were some important weaknesses of the Weimar political system:

- First, the president had the ability to use emergency powers in times of difficulty; this was Article 48 of the constitution. This was a problem as it could be abused.
- Second, the proportional representation system for voting in the *Reichstag* meant it was difficult to create majority governments and there was more chance of coalitions forming.
- In the early years of the Weimar Republic there was a great deal of political instability, as demonstrated by the Spartacist Uprising of January 1919 and the Kapp Putsch of March 1920.
- After the difficulties of 1923 (see 'Economic factors', below), the Weimar Republic was able to strengthen politically; this was in large part due to the improved economic conditions. However, many Germans felt dissatisfied with democracy and coalition governments.

■ Economic factors

Economic conditions were difficult after the war, including high levels of war debt and unemployment. Germany faced a huge reparations bill as part of the Treaty of Versailles:

- By April 1921, the final sum of money that Germany had to pay had been agreed on at £6.6 billion. The increasing demands for reparations payments caused problems for the already weakened German economy, contributing to both the French invasion of the Ruhr and the worsening hyperinflation crisis of 1923.
- In the mid- to late-1920s, the German economy improved because of better fiscal policies and improving international relations. This period is known as the Golden Age of Weimar and is often associated with the policies of Chancellor Gustav Stresemann, who introduced a new currency and secured foreign investments in Germany.
- It must be noted that not all Germans benefited from this Golden Age. Many people were ruined by the hyperinflation crisis. Farmers also experienced difficulties during this time.
- For the most part though, there was more prosperity. However, the Wall Street Crash of 1929 changed this situation, leading to the onset of economic depression in Germany. The crash led to the recalling of American loans taken on by German businesses during the Golden Years, subsequently having a dire effect on the economy.

Hitler's rise to power

- The depression led to very high unemployment and the closing of businesses. Unemployment increased from 1.7 million in 1929 to over 8 million in 1933.
- Evidence suggests that the Nazis were able to benefit from these economic problems as their share of the vote increased as a result of the depression.
- This interpretation suggests that due to the difficulties people were experiencing, the appeal of Nazism would increase.

POLITICAL STRUCTURE OF WEIMAR

Check your understanding of the Weimar Republic by filling in the following table. A selection of possible answers is written underneath.

	Role 1	Role 2	Role 3
The voters			
The president			
The chancellor and ministers			
The *Reichstag*			
The *Reichsrat*			

A selection of possible answers:

- Can advise the chancellor on the passing of new laws.
- All men and women over the age of twenty.
- They vote for the *Reichstag* every four years.
- Appoints and dismisses the chancellor.
- Can use Article 48 to pass emergency laws.
- They vote for the president every seven years.
- Controls the armed forces.
- Runs the government offices.
- Is democratically elected.
- They vote on laws.
- Seat holders are called deputies.
- Proposes new laws to the *Reichstag*.
- Has the power of veto over the introduction of new laws.

SPIDER DIAGRAM

Create a spider diagram to summarize the conditions in Germany prior to the rise to power of Adolf Hitler and the establishment of the Nazi state. You can use this template to help you to do this.

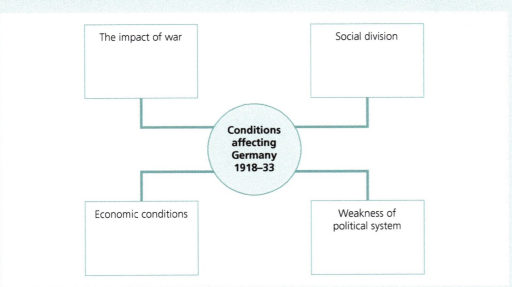

Methods by which states emerged

There is no doubt that the conditions Germany experienced as a result of the First World War, as well as the economic and political conditions during the Weimar years, helped the Nazis gain power. However, this interpretation also needs to consider the role played by Adolf Hitler and the Nazi Party themselves. We can see a range of factors which would suggest that the Nazis used a range of methods to place themselves in a more favourable position.

The use of force

- Early on, the Nazis used violence to intimidate and get their views across to people. The military arm of the party was the **Sturmabteilung (SA)**, led by **Ernst Röhm**. This group provided security to the party during rallies, as well as attacking communists in Germany.
- The Nazis' first attempt at power, the **Munich *Putsch*** in November 1923, involved the use of force. Hitler believed that the conditions were right for a bid for power due to the severe hyperinflation crisis that was affecting Germany. He also felt that the Nazi Party had enough popular support.
- Organized in alliance with General **Ludendorff**, the *putsch* was an uprising in Munich where around 2000 people, in support of the Nazis, marched into the centre of the city.
- The *putsch* failed, the police shot at the marchers and it fell apart. The *putsch* led to Hitler's imprisonment at **Landsberg Prison**.
- After the failure of the *putsch*, Hitler favoured political means to gain power through methods that would increase the Nazis' share of the vote in elections. However, violence was still present, and the SA played a role in intimidating opposition and carrying out anti-Semitic attacks.
- Prior to the establishment of the Nazi state, the **Schutzstaffel (SS)** had been formed. **Heinrich Himmler** had been appointed leader of this group.

SOURCE INVESTIGATION

Consider the sources and complete the accompanying questions.

SOURCE 3

The percentage of the vote secured by the NSDAP from 1928 to 1932. Data adapted from the Marxists Internet Archive (available at www.marxists.org/archive/trotsky/germany/elect.htm).

Year	Percentage of the vote
May 1928	2.6%
September 1930	18.3%
July 1932	37.4%
November 1932	33.1%

3 In what ways do the statistics in Source 3 suggest that the Nazis' popularity was in direct relation to the impact of the depression?

4 What evidence can you find in Source 4 to explain the drop in vote between July and November 1932?

SOURCE 4

Extract from Laurence Rees, *The Nazis: A Warning From History*, BBC Books, London, 2003, page 40.

The Nazi Party's popularity appeared to have peaked in the summer of 1932. Its support was inherently unstable, the party held together more by emotion and notions of its leader's charisma than by any coherent manifesto of concrete policy. Its rapid growth in popularity owed much to the crisis in which Germany found herself and over which the Nazis had no control. If the German economy began to pick up, success could vanish as rapidly as it had appeared, and the signs were that the economy was about to improve given the political agreement at the Lausanne Conference in June 1932 that effectively ended the reparations payments.

5 What perspective is provided in Source 4? What do you think might be the values and limitations of this view?

REFLECTING ON SIGNIFICANCE

Go through the following conditions in Germany prior to 1933 and reflect on why they are significant to the rise to power of the Nazis.

Conditions facing Germany	Why would this be significant to the rise to power of the Nazis?
High levels of unemployment during the depression in Germany	
Proportional representation voting system leading to regular coalition governments	
Popularity of the Communist Party (KPD) throughout the years of the Weimar Republic	
Political and economic instability during the early years of the Weimar Republic	

Leaders

In the early 1920s, Hitler quickly established himself as a leader within the party. Hitler made numerous speeches in beer halls, often with a popular reception. He would talk about a range of political views including German nationalism, anti-Semitism, anti-communism, and anger around the circumstances of the end of the First World War and the Treaty of Versailles:

- Hitler soon became an influential member of the party and the party formally made demands for how Germany should change if they were to gain political power. This included the unity of German people, abolition of the Treaty of Versailles, an expansionist foreign policy to gain more territory and no Jewish German citizens.
- This **25-Point Programme** was announced in 1920 and was a clear indication of the basis of Nazi ideology.

Hitler's authority as leader was challenged after he decided that the Nazis would need to use political means in order to gain power, rather than force. This view came after the failed Munich *Putsch*:

- One main challenge came from the brothers **Otto Strasser** and **Gregor Strasser**, who felt that the party needed to move towards socialism, advocating strikes and more state control of industries throughout Germany.
- This left-wing faction came into conflict with Hitler and his supporters. Hitler felt that they needed to work with Germany's big business owners and industrialists. The Strasser brothers were eventually defeated in 1930.
- During the rise to power of Hitler, there were many other prominent Nazis who played different roles in the party. These included **Hermann Göring**, **Joseph Goebbels** and Heinrich Himmler, who would all go on to have roles within the Nazi government once they were in power.

Ideology

- After the failure of the Munich *Putsch*, Hitler used his trial as an opportunity to promote his views, gaining a sympathetic ear from the judge and subsequently receiving a lenient prison sentence.
- Hitler wrote **Mein Kampf** while in prison, which would be used to help define the Nazis' ideological position. This included anti-Semitism, anti-communism, racial superiority of **Aryans** and traditional gender roles within society.
- **Lebensraum** was an idea promoted by Hitler that called for German expansionism to allow Germany to have more 'living space'. He also sought to unite all German-speaking people.
- The ideology also stressed the importance of German economic self-sufficiency, or **autarky**. This was probably a result of the economic depression in Germany where the reliance on American loans had weakened the economy.
- Also, importantly, Nazi ideology promoted the view of strong leadership, and as seen once in power, the dismantling of democracy.

THE NAZI PARTY'S PROGRAMME

An early indication of Nazi ideology can be seen in the 25-Point Programme. Go through a selection of the points and reflect on why these different policies and ideological positions would make the Nazis more or less appealing to different sections of society. Two answers have been done for you already and are annotated on the source.

SOURCE 5

Simplified extract of the basic programme of the National Socialist German Workers' Party (known as the 25-Point Programme), quoted in Office of the United States Chief Counsel for Prosecution of Axis Criminality, *Nazi Conspiracy and Aggression Volume IV*, United States Government Printing Office, Washington, DC, 1946.

1. The unification of all Germans.
2. Equal rights for German people and removal of the Treaties of Versailles and St Germain.
3. Land and territory for the German people.
4. Only Germans can be citizens. Jews cannot be German citizens.
5. Non-Germans can only visit the country as guests.
6. The right to vote is for German citizens only.
7. The economic and social rights of German citizens are the first priority.
8. No further immigration of non-Germans into the country. Foreigners who have moved to Germany since 1914 must be expelled. — *This would appeal to xenophobic attitudes in Germany at the time. It is also a clear indication of intolerance and discrimination that would be unpopular with many people.*
9. Citizens have equal rights and duties.
10. The first obligation of citizens is to work.
11. Removal of unemployment benefits.
12. War profits must be shared.
13. The nationalization of industries.
14. Profits from large industries must be shared.
15. Pensions must be provided and improved. — *This would be likely to be popular with many people, especially older people.*
16. Small businesses must be helped.
17. Changes in land distribution to help farmers.
18. To tackle seriously criminals and usurers [those who lend money at an unreasonably high rate of interest] who threaten national interest, they can be punished by death.
19. Reforms to the law.
20. Improve education for all German citizens regardless of income.
21. Improve national health by encouraging physical fitness.
22. The creation of a national army.
23. German press should be free from foreign influence.
24. Freedom of religion and encouragement of Christianity.
25. Central government needs sufficient power and authority to carry out any required changes.

3 Germany under Adolf Hitler, 1933–45

■ Persuasion, coercion and propaganda

We can see the role of persuasion and coercion throughout Hitler's rise to power as a technique to gain supporters. Hitler's speeches played a vital role in this process, and he was able to tailor his speeches to different sections of society to increase the popular appeal of the party:

- During the depression, speeches could be used to promote the Nazi solution to society's problems. For example, unemployed people may have seen a chance for work and a better life under the Nazis. Landowners and industrialists felt that their interests would be protected under the Nazis, probably taking assurance from the strong anti-communist and nationalist position. Hitler's continued attacks on the Treaty of Versailles also worked to coerce supporters.
- These techniques became more organized in the later stages of the 1920s as the Nazi Party started to use a more methodical system of propaganda to get its message across. Joseph Goebbels was in charge of the propaganda effort.
- Propaganda, such as the use of posters, leaflets, publications and radio broadcasts, was used to promote Hitler's election campaigns. Technology was also used, for example the 'Hitler Over Germany' campaign in 1932 where he flew to different cities all over the country to campaign for votes.

■ Circumstances leading to Hitler taking power

- A number of coalition governments were set up in the 1930s under the chancellorships of **Heinrich Brüning** (1930–2), **Franz von Papen** (1932) and **Kurt von Schleicher** (December 1932 to January 1933). Throughout this time, Paul von Hindenburg was president of the Weimar Republic.
- The Nazis throughout these years had increased their share of the vote and Hindenburg was under increased pressure to offer Hitler a position in the government.
- Hitler was eventually offered the position of vice-chancellor in August 1932 under von Papen, which Hitler refused. Hitler wanted a more influential role in the government.
- Hitler's response was to run for the presidency against Hindenburg in March and April 1932, which Hitler lost despite gaining a sizeable share of the vote.
- Furthermore, election results for the party as a whole in July 1932 demonstrated the continued popularity of the Nazis.
- Eventually, on the suggestion of von Papen, Hitler was appointed chancellor by Hindenburg in January 1933. The interpretation here is that von Papen and Hindenburg thought that they would be more able to control Hitler if he was in office. Von Papen infamously stated that 'he will have squeezed Hitler into a corner until he squeaks'.

■ Interpreting Hitler's rise to power

Historians have debated the factors leading to Hitler's rise to power throughout the twentieth century and through to today. It must be noted that these arguments need not be seen as distinct from each other. The table below summarizes a small selection of interpretations.

Perspectives on Nazism	Explanation
Sonderweg (special path)	This theory suggests that Germany went through a unique set of stages in its history which culminated in the rise of Nazi Germany, drawing on the importance of militarism and nationalism in the past. A key proponent of this was William Shirer, who wrote *The Rise and Fall of the Third Reich* in 1960. The theory is criticized for having too many different factors at play to take this linear view. Some historians have suggested that there was a broader development at play during the interwar years which saw the rejection of democracy in multiple countries, not just Germany
Hitler as a strong leader	**Intentionalist** historians focus on the special role of Hitler in shaping both the Nazi Party and its ideology. They suggest that he was the central reason for both its rise to power and maintenance of power, often referring to his emotional appeal to the German people. This view takes the 'master planner' view of Hitler, suggesting that he was in control of the party machine and had a clear plan for the development of Germany
Functionalist	The functionalist (or structuralist) approach finds the overemphasis on Hitler too limiting, suggesting that an investigation of the entire Nazi system and administration is required to understand both the rise of Hitler and how the state operated. An early proponent of this view was **Hans Mommsen**, who saw Hitler as a 'weak dictator', challenging the established narratives about Hitler being the all-seeing-and-knowing leader

SOURCE 6

An extract about Adolf Hitler from Franz von Papen, *Memoirs*, André Deutsch, London, 1952, pages 259–60.

There was little hint of either domination or genius in his manner or appearance, but he had immense powers of persuasion and an extraordinary and indefinable capacity for bending individuals and, above all, the masses to his will. He was fully aware of this power and completely convinced of his infallibility.

SOURCE 7

Extract from William Shirer, *The Rise and Fall of the Third Reich*, Secker & Warberg, London, 1960, page 236.

It is difficult to understand the behavior of most German Protestants in the first Nazi years unless one is aware of two things: their history and the influence of Martin Luther. The great founder of Protestantism was both a passionate anti-Semite and a ferocious believer in absolute obedience to political authority. He wanted Germany rid of the Jews and when they were sent away he advised that they be deprived of 'all their cash and jewels and silver and gold' and, furthermore, 'that their synagogues or schools be set on fire, that their houses be broken up and destroyed … and they be put under a roof or stable, like the gypsies … in misery and captivity as they incessantly lament and complain to God about us' – advice that was literally followed four centuries later by Hitler, Goering and Himmler.

HITLER'S RISE TO POWER

Take a look at the possible explanations for Hitler's rise to power. Write down the values and limitations of these perspectives from your own understanding. You can use Sources 6 and 7 to develop your ideas further about different perspectives.

Explanation	Values	Limitations
Hitler's rise to power was due to his unique abilities as a leader and emotional appeal to people in Germany		
Hitler's rise to power was due to the economic conditions facing Germany in the early 1930s, which ultimately favoured the rise of extremists		
Hitler's rise to power was the result of Germany's historical development over time, with a tradition of authority and distrust of democracy		
Hitler's rise to power should be viewed in the broader context of a global move towards authoritarian states as evidenced in Italy, Spain and Japan		

REVIEW YOUR UNDERSTANDING

Reflect on the relative importance of the different conditions and methods for the emergence of Hitler and the Nazis by 1933. Give each condition and method a score from 0 to 5 (with 5 being the most significant). Consider the reasons for your scores.

Conditions	Your score out of 5	Methods	Your score out of 5
War		Force	
Economics		Leaders	
Political system		Persuasion and coercion	
Social division		Propaganda	
		Ideology	

3 Germany under Adolf Hitler, 1933–45

Hitler's consolidation and maintenance of power

In January 1933, despite being chancellor, Hitler's position was far from secure. However, in just over a year he was declared as the *Führer* of Germany. Following this, the Nazis went on to implement a range of policies that promoted both popular support and fear in order to maintain the authority of the regime.

Initial consolidation: from chancellor to *Führer*

Steps to power:

Step 1: the *Reichstag* Fire
- Shortly after Hitler was appointed chancellor, the *Reichstag* building was set alight. The **Reichstag Fire** occurred on 27 February 1933 and a Dutch communist, **Marinus van der Lubbe**, was accused, convicted and executed for the arson.
- The Nazis used this as an opportunity to remove the communists as a source of opposition to their authority. Hitler persuaded Hindenburg to pass a decree that suspended civil liberties, which subsequently led to the arrest and imprisonment of many communists. It also led to the banning of communist groups' right to assembly and publish.

Step 2: the Enabling Act
- The results of the March 1933 election saw the Nazis increase their share of the vote to 43.91%, winning 288 seats. However, this was 36 seats short of a majority, so the Nazis were forced to form a coalition government with the **German National People's Party (DNVP)**.
- Hitler immediately prepared to pass a law called the **Enabling Act**. Alongside his coalition partners, Hitler persuaded politicians representing middle-class interests to vote in favour of the Act, including the Catholic Centre Party. Some politicians were intimidated to vote in favour.
- The Enabling Act was passed on 24 March 1933. The Act effectively allowed Hitler to pass legislation without consulting the *Reichstag*. Within months, all other political parties had been banned in Germany.
- After the passing of the Enabling Act, Hitler proceeded with a process known as **Gleichschaltung**, which involved a range of measures to consolidate the Nazi control over Germany. This included banning trade unions, political consolidation, removing Jewish people from governmental positions and beginning the process of controlling churches.
- Of note was the **Reichkonkordat** (more commonly referred to as the Concordat) between the German government and the **Holy See** in July 1933. This was an agreement that guaranteed freedoms for the Catholic Church in Germany in exchange for non-interference in Nazi policies.

Step 3: the Night of the Long Knives and the death of Hindenburg
- The **Night of the Long Knives** happened between 30 June and 2 July 1934. It was essentially a purge of any sources of opposition within the Nazi Party as well as attacks on any individuals who had stood against Hitler in the past.
- Most notably, this included the execution of Ernst Röhm, the head of the SA. He was accused of plotting a coup against Hitler and he was shot during the purge after he had refused to shoot himself. It also led to the rounding up of many members of the SA and their disbanding as a paramilitary organization.
- Other individuals who were killed included Gregor Strasser, who had previously opposed Hitler, and Kurt von Schleicher, the former chancellor.
- The event is significant as it showed the lengths to which Hitler was willing to go in the treatment of those he felt were in opposition to him.
- Later, on 2 August 1934, President Hindenburg died. Hitler then consolidated the office of president and chancellor into one, becoming the *Führer* of the Third Reich with the army swearing an oath of loyalty to him.
- The oath sworn by the army was important to Hitler's consolidation of power. Having control of the army was essential to his maintenance of power. Hitler later took personal command over the armed forces during the Second World War.

CREATE A TIMELINE

To aid your understanding of the early stages of Hitler's consolidation of power, create a short timeline of Hitler's consolidation of power. You should include the following events and details on the timeline:

- appointment of Hitler as chancellor
- passing of the Enabling Act
- *Reichstag* Fire
- March elections of 1933
- Night of the Long Knives
- Concordat
- death of Hindenburg

SUPPORT OR CHALLENGE?

Go through the following events, indicating whether each event supported or challenged Adolf Hitler's consolidation of power between 1933 and 1934.

Event	Support or challenge?	Explanation
Reichstag Fire		
March 1933 Elections		
Enabling Act		
Concordat with the Catholic Church		
Night of the Long Knives		
Oath of loyalty from the army		

Methods for the consolidation and maintenance of power

Use of force

The Night of the Long Knives is a clear example of the Nazis' use of force in order to consolidate their power. Throughout the Nazi regime, force was a major factor in maintaining control over the German people. One major body of control was the SS, which effectively worked as a police force throughout the country, often using illegal methods to intimidate and silence opposition:

- The SS was the organization that set up and ran the **concentration camps**, which were used to hold different groups of people targeted by the Nazis, including political opponents.
- The SS became the national police force by 1936 under the control of Heinrich Himmler. This was different from the system previously used, where police forces operated at a local level.
- One branch of the SS of note was the **Gestapo**, which operated as a secret police force that investigated suspected opponents throughout Germany. It was set up initially by Hermann Göring in 1933, but later came under the overall control of Himmler.
- The *Gestapo* used torture as a method to extract information from people. The *Gestapo* often held suspects without trial and a large number of people simply disappeared after being arrested.
- The *Gestapo* relied on ordinary people to denounce others to help create a more fearful atmosphere in the country.

Treatment of opposition

- The Nazi Party was able to operate without serious opposition for most of its rule over Germany.
- The far-reaching effects of the Enabling Act and the Night of the Long Knives enabled the Nazis to weaken potential opposition from the start.
- They also set up concentration camps that were used to imprison opponents to their rule. Early on in the Nazis' rule these opponents included many socialists and communists. The first concentration camp was set up in **Dachau** in March 1933.
- The use of the SS to maintain control of people throughout the country worked as a deterrent to potential opposition.
- There is also the argument that many people did not oppose the Nazis as their policies benefited them. This suggests that for many, Hitler was a popular leader and many people did not want to be in opposition.

Political opposition

- Political opposition could have come from socialist and communist groups, but their ability to co-ordinate was repressed early in the Nazi regime. Thousands of members of the SPD and the KPD were imprisoned in concentration camps. The remaining communists hid from the authorities, distributing leaflets as a form of opposition.
- In addition, the removal of trade unions made opposition from workers' groups difficult to organize. There was some low-level resistance from workers through strike action, refusing to perform the Nazi salute and sometimes sabotage of factory machines.

Opposition from the army

- A potentially strong source of opposition came from the military. This became more organized as the Second World War progressed and many officers became increasingly dissatisfied with Hitler's leadership.
- Opposition included the **Kreisau Circle**, made up of high-ranking military officers and members of the old aristocracy. They were behind the **July Bomb Plot** of 1944 when Colonel **Claus von Stauffenberg** attempted to assassinate Hitler with a bomb. The plot, despite injuring Hitler, failed and the leaders were executed.

CREATE A REVISION DIAGRAM

Create a revision diagram on the types of opposition that existed in Nazi Germany and the methods of treatment of opposition. You can use this template to help to structure your ideas.

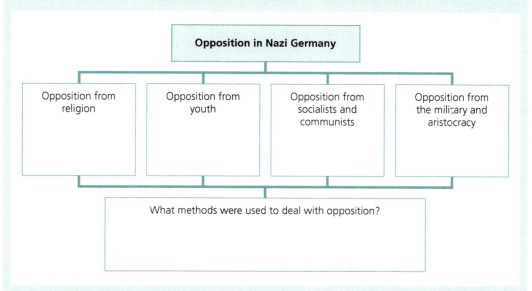

SOURCE 8

Extract from the Edelweiss Pirates song, quoted in Detlev J.K. Peukert, *Inside Nazi Germany*, translated by Richard Deveson, Yale University Press, New Haven, 1987, page 158.

Hark the hearty fellows sing!
Strum that banjo, pluck that string!
And the lassies all join in.
We're going to get rid of Hitler,
And he can't do a thing.

…

Hitler's power may lay us low,
And keep us locked in chains,
But we will smash the chains one day,
We'll be free again.
We've got fists and we can fight,
We've got knives and we'll get them out.
We want freedom, don't we boys?
We're the fighting Navajos.

…

We march by banks of Ruhr and Rhine
And smash the Hitler Youth in twain
Our song is freedom, love and life,
We're Pirates of the Edelweiss.

6   What can you learn about the perspectives of the Edelweiss Pirates from the lyrics of this song?

Opposition from youth

- Opposition from youth was usually on moral grounds or due to demands for more individual freedoms.
- The **White Rose** group was set up in moral opposition to many of the Nazis' policies that were felt to be inhumane, such as the Nazi euthanasia programme (see page 52) which included the murder of a number of mentally and physically disabled people.
- The White Rose leaders, **Hans Scholl** and **Sophie Scholl**, distributed leaflets in opposition to the Nazis but were eventually caught and executed by guillotine in 1943.
- Other youth groups included the **Edelweiss Pirates**, **Swing Youth** and the **Navajos**. They opposed the Nazis' authoritarian measures, especially the Hitler Youth. The Swing Youth wanted to listen to the banned jazz music and pursue freedoms that were restricted in Germany at the time.

Opposition from religious groups

As an important institution of German society and culture, the Church could have played an important role in opposition to the Nazis. However, on the most part we see compliance and muted opposition. There were some individual examples of opposition through religion:

- Individuals who opposed the Nazis included **Dietrich Bonhoeffer**, **Clemens von Galen**, **Martin Niemöller** and **Bernhard Lichtenberg**. They all spoke out against Nazi policies on a moral and religious basis. Hitler was careful in his treatment of religious opposition but eventually all of these religious leaders were either imprisoned in concentration camps or executed.
- Martin Niemöller had set up the **Confessional Church**, which was a more organized form of resistance. He was arrested and imprisoned for this.
- One interpretation of why more religious leaders did not oppose Nazis was that they liked the harsh treatment of communism in German society, viewing that ideology as more threatening to religious institutions.

Charismatic leadership and the dissemination of propaganda

There is little doubt that Hitler was a popular leader in Germany for many ordinary people. He was seen as the solution to many of the problems faced by the country in the years following the First World War and the depression. The reduction in unemployment and the gradual overturning of the Treaty of Versailles made many feel that Germany was becoming stronger. His image and words were used in propaganda to promote these messages further:

- The Ministry of Propaganda was set up in 1933 with Goebbels in charge.
- Outsiders were identified and were to be represented in a negative and discriminatory way; these included Jewish people, gay/lesbian people, Sinti and Roma people.
- A weekly newspaper, *Der Stümer*, was used to spread Nazi ideology, including anti-Semitism.
- Goebbels especially liked to use films to spread propaganda. Famous films included *Triumph of the Will* by **Leni Riefenstahl**, which showed the massive Nazi rallies at Nuremberg. Other films were extremely anti-Semitic, including *The Eternal Jew* and *Süss the Jew*, which were both made in 1940.
- All other available media (for example, photography, literature, music, books) was used to spread Nazi ideology and promote the role of Hitler and his cult of personality.
- Censorship was used widely; there were public book burnings of banned materials. Banned artists and authors included Pablo Picasso, Claude Monet, Karl Marx, Friedrich Engels and Sigmund Freud.

MIND MAP ON NAZI PROPAGANDA

Using the sources and your own knowledge, create a mind map on the different types of propaganda that were used in Nazi Germany. Include a range of examples. You can use Sources 9–11 to help you to complete this activity.

SOURCE 9

Extract from a speech by Joseph Goebbels, 'Our *Führer*', 1936, an annual speech made by the propaganda minister on the eve of Hitler's birthday (available at http://research.calvin.edu/german-propaganda-archive/unser36.htm).

Tomorrow morning, this whole people wishes to proclaim its love and honor to the Führer, but also its thankfulness for his impact on humanity and on history. Among them are those countless millions who cast their votes for him on 29 March of this year, and thus ceremonially affirmed that they saw him as the embodiment of faith in our national future, and of the security and honor of the Reich. Never before in history has one man so embodied the confidence and feeling of togetherness of a whole people. I am happy that tonight I am the interpreter of all these feelings.

We are still in the midst of the Führer's constructive work. Each of us has enough troubles and challenges to face, and there are countless tasks that confront us. And, of course, Adolf Hitler has not resolved all the tensions and differences, all the misunderstandings and frictions within the German people. But on this we can all agree: that Germany's leadership is in the best, most loyal and most dependable hands of Adolf Hitler, and that in him, in his person, and in his human and political impact, there is the assurance that these remaining problems will in good time find an appropriate organic solution. Like a rock in the ocean, he stands firm against all the troubles and difficulties of everyday life, the peaceful place in the flood of events.

SOURCE 10

A photograph of a Nazi rally, 16 September 1935. Hitler salutes Nazis as they march past during a parade in Nuremberg.

SOURCE 11

A cheerful group of Nazi troops and students gather seized papers and books to burn in the Opernplatz in Berlin on 10 May 1933.

Hitler's foreign policies

Hitler was well known for his aggressive foreign policy, which ultimately was the major cause of the Second World War. In this section, the role of foreign policy between 1933 and 1939 will be examined to consider its relative importance in Hitler's maintenance of power.

Aims of foreign policy

The intentionalist/functionalist debate has focused on Nazi foreign policy, with the debate discussing whether Hitler was a master planner or an opportunist with regard to foreign policy. Hitler's broad aims, as seen in Nazi ideology, were the uniting of German people, the overthrow of the Treaty of Versailles and the pursuit of *lebensraum* (living space), and we can see evidence of success in these aims.

Early foreign policy, 1933–6

Many of the foreign policy achievements of Nazi Germany were directed at overturning different aspects of the Treaty of Versailles. Hitler's success in doing this increased his popularity among the German people. Hitler's achievements included:

- Germany's withdrawal from the League of Nations in October 1933.
- The **Saarland** being returned to Germany in 1935 as a result of a **plebiscite** where the people voted in favour of being part of Germany rather than France.
- The rearmament of Germany from 1935 onwards, in direct violation of the Treaty of Versailles. The army was expanded and conscription was introduced.
- Sending troops to the **Rhineland**, which was supposed to be a demilitarized region as stipulated in the Treaty of Versailles. The troops entered the region and there was little opposition from either France or Britain.
- The limited responses of Britain and France gave Hitler the confidence to pursue more and more ambitious foreign policy moves. This can be seen in the years leading up to the Second World War.

Steps to war, 1936–9

In the years leading up to war, Hitler's foreign policy moves sought to further reinforce his position and expand German territory and influence. He sent troops to support Franco in the **Spanish Civil War**. Hitler developed allies in 1936, working closely with **Benito Mussolini** of Italy and the militarist government of Japan, signing the Anti-Comintern Pact in November. Gradually, his actions became more aggressive, leading to the outbreak of war in September 1939:

- In 1938, Germany and Austria united in the **Anschluss**. This had been the wish of the Austrian Nazi Party, and Germany's armed forces were given a warm welcome by the Austrian people when they marched into Austria to begin the process. A plebiscite was held, with the majority of people voting for the union. This was a high point for Hitler given his Austrian nationality.
- Later in 1938, Hitler was able to take over the **Sudetenland** in Czechoslovakia. This was not achieved as easily as the *Anschluss* and the Czechoslovakian government was in fierce opposition to this. Despite the opposition, Hitler achieved his objectives. This was due to the outcomes of the Munich Conference in October 1938, where Britain, France and Italy voted in favour of Hitler's demands.
- In 1939, Hitler took things a step further with demands for the return of former German territory that was now in Poland. The British and French opposed this: war was declared in September of that year.
- The signing of the Nazi–Soviet Pact in August 1939 was a peculiar occurrence given the earlier Anti-Comintern Pact and the Nazis' anti-communist ideology. The agreement meant that Hitler would not have to worry about the Soviet Union while he pursued an invasion of Poland and, later, war in Western Europe.

Hitler's consolidation and maintenance of power

ESSAY PLANNING

7 In what ways did foreign policy affect the rule of two authoritarian leaders, each from a different region?

Create an essay plan for this question. Go through the following checklist to help you to plan your answer:

- What is the command term? How will this affect the structure and focus of your essay?
- Which authoritarian rulers will you choose to focus on? Are they the best examples for this particular question?
- What do you want to say in your introduction, body paragraphs and conclusions? Make a rough plan as to your line of argument throughout.
- What facts can you use to support your argument and analysis?

There are a few different approaches you can take with this question. You could choose to write comparatively about the two leaders together, focusing on examples of foreign policy success and failure. Alternatively, you could write about each leader in turn and then make some overall comparative and concluding statements.

HITLER'S FOREIGN POLICY

Consider Hitler's foreign policy from 1933 to 1939. In what ways had he achieved his aims? The sources on this page can help you. Use the table below as a template.

Aims of Hitler's foreign policy	Successes	Failures
Dismantling the Treaty of Versailles		
Uniting German-speaking people		
Lebensraum		

SOURCE 12

German military resources, quoted in John Hite and Chris Hinton, *Weimar and Nazi Germany*, Hodder Education, London, 2000.

Year	Soldiers	Aircraft
1932	100,000	36
1939	950,000	8250

SOURCE 13

A map showing the territorial gains of Nazi Germany up until 1939.

Hitler's domestic policies: aims and results

Hitler's economic policies

One of Hitler's chief economic aims was autarky; this means economic independence or self-sufficiency. However, Hitler was no economic planner and left the running of the economy to different individuals, including **Hjalmar Schacht**, who was the minister of economics from 1934 to 1937. Schacht was succeeded by Hermann Göring, who took the economy in a different direction, one which was far more aligned to Hitler's wishes for autarky and rearmament. Finally, **Albert Speer** oversaw the war economy in the closing years of the Second World War.

Schacht and the New Plan

- By the time Hitler took office the depression was easing globally and he was able to associate himself with the recovery.
- The minister of economics was Hjalmar Schacht, a well-connected banker and economist who wanted to promote the growth of German industry, improve the **balance of trade** and reduce unemployment.
- As well as co-ordinating big business and industry to work together through the creation of the **Organization of Industry**, he introduced policies to reduce the high levels of unemployment in Germany.
- These included the creation of **public works schemes**. These involved the building of a wide range of infrastructure projects such as **autobahns**, schools, hospitals and other public buildings.
- In 1934, the **National Labour Force (RAD)** was set up. This was made up of young men who were sent to work on different work schemes as well as being taught new skills.
- These policies saw the unemployment figures fall drastically during the 1930s; however, it must be noted that women and Jewish people were not included in the statistics.
- Schacht's main problem was the balance of trade, in that Germany had higher imports than exports. His **New Plan** of 1934 addressed this problem with tighter import controls. Schacht was also able to negotiate bilateral trade deals.

Göring and rearmament

- Another of Hitler's chief aims was rearmament. He felt that the pace for achieving this was too slow under Schacht, so, by 1936, Hermann Göring, commander-in-chief of the **Luftwaffe**, was tasked with pushing Germany in this direction.
- The difference of opinion between Schacht and Göring can be seen in the **Guns or Butter** debate, where butter refers to consumer goods and guns to rearmament.
- Göring, favouring guns, introduced the **Four-Year Plan**, which included an expansion of arms manufacturing, tight import controls and the development of domestic industries.
- Developing domestic industries was an attempt to find or create replacements for imported goods to increase self-sufficiency. The replacements were known as **ersatz goods**. Despite the achievements, Germany still relied heavily on imports by 1939.

Speer and the war economy

Through the course of the Second World War the economy was put on a strict war footing. By 1942, Albert Speer was put in charge as minister of armaments. He was able to co-ordinate factories and industries effectively to support the needs of the war by a range of strict controls and by limiting freedoms.

SUCCESS OR FAILURE?

Using the information on page 48 and the sources, reflect on the relative successes and failures of Nazi economic policy.

Aims	Success?	Failure?
Recovery from the economic depression		
Self-sufficiency (autarky)		
Rearmament		

SOURCE 14

Unemployment figures in Germany from 1932 to 1938, quoted in John Hite and Chris Hinton, *Weimar and Nazi Germany*, Hodder Education, London, 2000.

Year	Number unemployed
1932	5.6 million
1934	2.3 million
1936	1.6 million
1938	0.2 million

Public expenditure on rearmament in Germany between 1928 and 1938, quoted in John Hite and Chris Hinton, *Weimar and Nazi Germany*, Hodder Education, London, 2000.

Year	Expenditure (Reichsmarks)
1928	0.7 billions
1932	0.7 billions
1934	3.0 billions
1938	17.2 billions

SOURCE 15

A photograph from 1933 showing Adolf Hitler breaking ground on an *autobahn* in Frankfurt.

SOURCE 16

Extract from Geoff Layton, *Germany: The Third Reich 1933–45*, Hodder Education, London, 2005, page 40. Historian Geoff Layton explains the successes and failures of the Four-Year Plan.

The success of the Plan was mixed over the years. On the one hand, production of a number of key materials, such as aluminium and explosives, had expanded greatly, or at least at a reasonable rate. On the other hand, it fell a long way short of the targets in the essential commodities of rubber and oil, while arms production never reached the levels desired by the armed forces and Hitler. All in all, the Four-Year Plan had succeeded in the sense that Germany's reliance on imports had not increased. However, this still meant that when war did break out Germany was dependent on foreign supplies for one third of its raw materials.

Hitler's social policies

The social policies of the Nazis had far-reaching effects across different sections of society. Hitler wanted to create a *Volksgemeinschaft*, placing an emotional emphasis on the creation of a Germanic community of Aryans who were united in their aims. This section will look at the impact of Nazi policy on workers, youth, women and minority groups.

Impact on workers

- As we have already seen, Nazi economic policies led to a reduction in unemployment and many German workers found themselves working on public works schemes. Young men aged 18–25 were expected to spend six months in the RAD.
- Workers' rights were curtailed with the ban on trade unions in 1933, being replaced with the **German Labour Front (DAF)** to which every worker in the country belonged. This ensured tighter control over workers' rights and discipline.
- To offer incentives for hard work, the **Strength Through Joy** programme was launched to provide workers with rewards for their work. These included cheap holidays, leisure activities and opportunities for fitness training. The emphasis on health and fitness can be seen in the Nazis' racial policy, which focused on the Aryan people as the master race.
- Despite these rewards, workers' freedoms were more limited under the Nazis and for many people, working conditions were tougher under the Nazis than before.

Impact on youth

The Hitler Youth

- The main organization for young people was the **Hitler Youth**. It had existed as a youth wing of the Nazi Party since the 1920s but expanded throughout the country once the Nazis took power.
- The Hitler Youth was run by **Baldur von Schirach**.
- The group wore uniforms with a swastika on the armband, carried flags and sang songs promoting Hitler and Nazi ideology.
- As a paramilitary organization, Hitler Youth meetings often involved training, which was a precursor to military training, including drills, outdoor survival skills and using weapons.
- Nazi ideology, especially concerning Aryan supremacy, was a major teaching of the organization and members were trained to identify the outsiders of society such as Jewish people and other minority groups.
- By 1939, membership was compulsory, with around 8 million boys belonging to the Hitler Youth by this time.
- For girls, the **League of German Maidens** was set up to carry out similar activities to the Hitler Youth but with more focus on domestic skills such as sewing and cooking.

Schools in Nazi Germany

- Schools were important places for the Nazi indoctrination of youth and all subjects were changed to promote Nazi values and ideology.
- The head of the Ministry of Education was **Bernhard Rust**.
- Within schools, **eugenics** was taught to promote Aryan supremacy. Students were also indoctrinated in anti-Semitism, often from a young age. A book for children at the time was ***The Poisonous Mushroom***, which depicted Jewish people in a highly negative manner.
- Physical education was prioritized, with students taking more exercise classes.
- History was rewritten to celebrate Germany's achievements in the past as well as to demonize the issues surrounding the end of the First World War and the Treaty of Versailles.
- Controls were placed on teachers; Jewish teachers lost their jobs early on. Teachers were expected to fully embrace National Socialism ideology when dealing with students.
- Nazi elite schools, known as ***Napolas***, were also set up for eligible students and were run by the SS. They were designed to train a future generation of government and military leaders. The main focus was on physical exercise and fitness.

DOMESTIC POLICIES AND YOUNG PEOPLE

8 Examine the successes and failures of domestic policy in one authoritarian state.

Read the following extracts that are in response to the essay question above that discuss the impact of domestic policy on young people. As you read through the extracts, make a note of the strengths and limitations of the responses.

SAMPLE 1

A major target for the creation of the *Volksgemeinschaft* was the conformity and support of young people across Germany. Younger people were, understandably, viewed as the future of Germany and a variety of policies sought to indoctrinate and teach them the values that were in line with Nazi ideology.

Schools are a clear example of this. Widespread propaganda and censorship extended into the field of education and textbooks used across the different subjects had to be rewritten to fit in with the Nazi world view. For example, the history class taught a version of the past that fit in with Nazi nostalgia for the past and a demonization of the circumstances surrounding the end of the First World War. Physical education was encouraged, playing a far more prominent role in the day-to-day schedules of students, this was in line with the Aryan/master race dogma which sought to train young people to become more physically fit. Racism was also taught through the study of eugenics, which was a corrupt race science that sought to indoctrinate younger people into believing the propaganda of Aryan supremacy and increasing discrimination to others, especially Jewish people.

SAMPLE 2

Despite the range of policies directed towards young people as seen in the Hitler Youth and the changes affecting school, there was opposition to the Nazis. This indicates that perhaps their policies were not so successful in changing the hearts and minds of young people. Opposition ranged from minor acts of rebellion, such as smoking cigarettes through to organized action against the Nazi state. A notable example of youth opposition to the Nazis can be viewed in the White Rose group who took a moral stance against the euthanasia programme that was used. Hans and Sophie Scholl worked to spread opposition on moral grounds to these programmes. Their arrest and later execution is evidence of the difficulties of trying to make a stand against the Nazis.

SOURCE 17

A propaganda poster for enrolment in the Hitler Youth, 1936.

9 What is the message of this propaganda poster?

Impact on women

- Women were not regarded as equal to men according to Nazi ideology. Hitler believed in distinct gender roles, with the emphasis for women on being home-makers and raising children.
- Women were represented by the **National Socialist Women's League**, which was subordinate to the Nazi Party.
- Women's rights became increasingly restricted, including reduced access to higher education and employment. Women were not allowed to join the civil service.
- Socially, women were encouraged to be healthy in their lifestyles. Smoking was discouraged, as was make-up.
- The slogan **Kinder, Küche, Kirche** (children, kitchen, church) summarized the Nazis' priorities for women.
- A major aim of social policy was to increase the birth rate; women were encouraged to have large families. Abortion was made illegal. Women were encouraged to have a 'child for Hitler', even outside marriage, which contradicted the initial aims of promoting the nuclear family as the place for raising children.
- During the Second World War, the position of women changed given the need to support the war effort. Many women were required to carry out national service for one year, working on farms as part of the Land Year Programme. After 1942, many women had to work in factories to support the war economy.
- An extreme policy carried out by the SS, under the directive of Himmler, was **Lebensborn** (spring of life), which sought to co-ordinate the increase in the birth of Aryans by choosing women to procreate with SS men, as well as arranging the adoption of orphans viewed to be racially pure.

Impact on minorities

The Nazi state was intolerant of many groups of people identified as 'outsiders' and they were subject to discrimination. The height of this intolerance culminated in the Holocaust, which led to the mass murder of over 6 million Jewish people.

Sterilization and euthanasia policies

- The Nazis carried out the sterilization of thousands of people, including many blind and deaf people.
- Euthanasia centres were also set up, which involved the forced killings of people viewed as unwanted by the Nazi regime. These included people suffering from mental illnesses. The deaths were covered up to keep the programme a secret.
- There was opposition to these policies but it was often repressed. Religious leaders spoke out against the policies, including Clemens von Galen who described them as 'moral depravity'.
- The euthanasia programme ended in 1941 due to its unpopularity and the moral outrage.

Hitler's domestic policies: aims and results

SOURCE INVESTIGATION

10 Read Source 18, the Nazi Ten Commandments for the choice of spouse, and find examples that highlight different aspects of Nazi ideology.

11 Using Source 19, explain a) gender roles in Nazi Germany and b) the impact that the Second World War had on this process.

SOURCE 18

The Nazi 'Ten Commandments for the choice of a spouse', quoted in J. Noakes and G. Pridham, editors, *Nazism, 1919–45*, volume 2, University of Exeter Press, Exeter, 1984, page 463.

1. Remember you are a German.
2. If you are genetically healthy you should not remain unmarried.
3. Keep your body pure.
4. Keep your mind and spirit pure.
5. As a German choose only a spouse of the same or Nordic blood.
6. In choosing a spouse ask about his ancestors.
7. Health is also a precondition for physical beauty.
8. Marry only for love.
9. Don't look for a playmate but for a companion for marriage.
10. You should want to have as many children as possible.

SOURCE 19

Extract from the United States Holocaust Memorial Museum, 'Women in the Third Reich', Holocaust Encyclopedia (available at www.ushmm.org/wlc/en/article.php?ModuleId=10005205).

The National Socialist Women's Union and German Women's Agency used Nazi propaganda to encourage women to focus on their roles as wives and mothers. Besides increasing the population, the regime also sought to enhance its 'racial purity' through 'species upgrading', notably by promulgating laws prohibiting marriage between 'Aryans' and 'non-Aryans' while preventing those with handicaps and certain diseases from marrying at all.

Girls were taught to embrace the role of mother and obedient wife in school and through compulsory membership in the Nazi League of German Girls. However, rearmament followed by total war obliged the Nazis to abandon the domestic ideal for women. The need for labor prompted the state to prod women into the workforce (for example, through the Duty Year, the compulsory-service plan for all women) and even into the military itself (the number of female auxiliaries in the German armed forces approached 500,000 by 1945).

REVISION QUESTIONS

As we reach the end of this topic, have a look through these questions to reflect on your understanding of this case study:

- In what ways would Germany's loss of the First World War have shaped Hitler's ideological beliefs?
- In what way did existing conditions favour the rise to power of the Nazi Party?
- What were the circumstances which led to Hitler's appointment as chancellor in 1933?
- What events were important to Hitler's early consolidation of power after 1933?
- What were the main economic aims of the Nazis? How successful were they in meeting these aims?
- What opposition existed in Nazi Germany and how was it dealt with?
- Summarize the impact of the Nazis on a) women, b) religion and c) minorities.
- What was meant by the term 'Working towards the *Führer*'?
- To what extent did Hitler achieve authoritarian control?

Treatment of Jewish people

From the outset we can see the high levels of discrimination towards Jewish people directed by Nazi policy. The following is a selection of examples of how these policies became increasingly severe as time passed.

General discrimination
- Early on in Nazi rule, Jewish people were not allowed to work in government jobs, including the civil service.
- Violence was also directed towards Jewish people in public.
- Jewish teachers were no longer allowed to work in schools.

The Nuremberg Laws
- The **Nuremberg Laws** provided a legal framework for discrimination. The laws were passed in 1935.
- The laws stated that Jewish people could not be German citizens, and there could be no sexual relations or marriage between Jewish people and German citizens. (See Source 20, page 55.)

Kristallnacht
- In 1938, discrimination increased further with increasingly repressive employment policies.
- A significant event in November was *Kristallnacht*, which was a co-ordinated number of attacks on Jewish houses, shops, businesses and synagogues.
- Although carried out by the Nazis, *Kristallnacht* led to the arrests of thousands of Jewish people and their imprisonment in concentration camps.

The 'Final Solution'
- The outbreak of the Second World War intensified the discrimination and, from 1939 onwards, killings became more common, especially in those areas of Europe occupied by the Nazis.
- At the **Wannsee Conference** in 1942, plans were made to put Jewish people in labour camps as well as the formulation of the death camps. This became known as the 'Final Solution'.
- From 1942 to 1945, what came to be called the **Holocaust** was carried out. This was the mass murder of millions of Jewish people in death camps. A system using gas chambers was set up to carry out this atrocity.

Treatment of other minority groups
- Other groups in Germany also experienced discrimination from the Nazis.
- These included Roma and Sinti people, gay/lesbian people, Jehovah's Witnesses and black Germans.
- From this we can see that there were extreme levels of racism, homophobia and religious intolerance. In the concentration camps, minorities were forced to wear a badge identifying them, for instance Jehovah's Witnesses wore a purple triangle.

Hitler's domestic policies: aims and results

NUREMBERG LAWS

Read the extract and then answer the question below.

SOURCE 20

First four articles of the Nuremberg Laws from 1935, quoted in Y. Arad, Y. Gutman and A. Margaliot, *Documents on the Holocaust: Selected Sources on the Destruction of the Jews of Germany and Austria, Poland, and the Soviet Union,* **Yad Vashem/Pergamon Press, Oxford, 1981, page 78.**

Article 1

1 Marriages between Jews and subjects of the state of German or related blood are forbidden. Marriages nevertheless concluded are invalid, even if concluded abroad to circumvent this law.

2 Annulment proceedings can be initiated only by the state prosecutor.

Article 2

Extramarital intercourse between Jews and subjects of the state of German or related blood is forbidden.

Article 3

Jews may not employ in their households female subjects of the state of German or related blood who are under 45 years old.

Article 4

1 Jews are forbidden to fly the Reich or National flag or display Reich colors.

2 They are, on the other hand, permitted to display the Jewish colors. The exercise of this right is protected by the State.

12 Using Source 20, describe the ways in which Jewish people were discriminated against by the introduction of the Nuremberg Laws.

_____
_____
_____
_____

13 Examine the impact of the policies of one authoritarian state on minority groups. Practise writing two paragraphs in response to this question, considering the different ways that minority groups were affected by the Nazi Party. You could use these sentence starters to help you:

From the outset, Nazi Germany was an ideologically intolerant state …

The treatment of minority groups became progressively worse through the rule of the Nazi Party.

For example …

SECTION 3 Exam focus

Sample question and answer

Read this student answer to the essay question. Consider the strengths and limitations of the response. Pay attention to the annotated comments. Write down what you like about the response and any suggestions for improvement.

Examine the role played by economic conditions in the rise to power of one authoritarian ruler.

> On 30 January 1933, Adolf Hitler was appointed as chancellor of Germany. He held power until his death in 1945. It can be suggested that Hitler's rise to power was aided by the economic conditions facing Germany. This can be seen in the lack of economic stability in the years following the First World War and the Weimar Republic, as well as in the severe economic environment of the depression during the early 1930s. However, it should also be considered that both existing political conditions and the actions of Hitler and the Nazi Party played a vital role in their rise to power.
>
> In the years following the First World War, Germany experienced a fair amount of economic uncertainty. The war had left the country weakened with large amounts of debt. Added to this, Germany also faced a huge reparations bill, stipulated under the terms of the Treaty of Versailles. These economic conditions contributed to an unstable society in the years after the war which provided a platform for Hitler to develop his political opinions and ideology. Much of his political rhetoric was a direct result of what he saw as injustices against Germany through the signing of both the armistice in 1918 and the Treaty of Versailles in 1919. Furthermore, the worsening economic situation in 1923 with the invasion of the Ruhr by the French and a severe hyperinflation crisis provided the conditions for the Nazi Party to take action with the attempted seizure of power in Munich in November of that year.
>
> However, these early economic conditions can be seen to be of lesser significance in the rise to power of Hitler and the Nazis as they did not directly place them into political power. In fact, after the failure of the Munich Putsch, the Nazis were still a small party with limited influence. The improving economic conditions from 1924 onwards further weakened the Nazi Party. The period of time from 1924 to 1929 is sometimes referred to as the 'Golden Years' as there seemed to be an upsurge in both the prosperity and mood of the country. During the peak of this era, the Nazis were only able to secure 2.8% of the vote, suggesting that economic conditions may in fact have a relationship with the appeal of more extreme political viewpoints.
>
> Perhaps the most convincing evidence that suggests that economic conditions played a vital role in the rise to power of the Nazis can be seen in the impact of the depression on Germany. In October 1929, the New York stock exchange crashed and this led to a global economic downturn. Germany was hit severely as much of the finance used to develop the economy had been through loans which were quickly recalled. Economic depression in Germany led to the closure of many businesses as well as spiralling unemployment. Most of German society was affected, with many people going hungry as they could no longer afford food. These conditions created a favourable situation for the Nazis to exploit to increase their political power. Through organized campaigns, with widespread use of propaganda, they were able to feed off people's anger and fears to make themselves more electable. This can be seen in the election results in the early 1930s, where the

The introduction provides a hook and a thesis which gives a clear indication of the direction that the essay is going.

The student uses historical concepts here.

Use of factual evidence through statistics.

Nazis increased their share of the vote from 18.3% in 1930 to 37.3% in the summer of 1932. These electoral gains were the major cause behind Hindenburg's decision to appoint Hitler as chancellor. Comparatively, we can see a similar process occurring in Japan at the time, a country that was also severely affected by the depression, as the 1930s saw an increase in support for militarist leaders who wanted to take the country away from democracy. *[Relevant point of comparison on how economic depression can lead to increase in the popularity of authoritarianism.]*

Subsequently, we can make a strong claim that economic conditions did contribute significantly to the rise to power of the Nazis. However, we must be aware that this interpretation is not complete, as it does not consider the importance of the methods used by the Nazis in their rise to power, such as their effective use of propaganda to spread their ideology, *[More examples could have been given to provide depth.]* or indeed other conditions facing Germany at that time, such as the ineffectiveness of the Weimar political system. *[Needs more explanation.]*

This answer is well written and the student has very good historical awareness of the time period prior to Hitler's rise to power. There is plenty of analysis and use of historical concepts. For development, a wider range of historical knowledge would help to improve the overall depth of the response.

Exam practice

Now either have a go at the above essay question or try one of the following questions, using Hitler as your case study.

1. Examine the impact of one authoritarian state on the people who lived under it.
2. Examine the circumstances that led to the emergence of one authoritarian state.
3. Examine the role of foreign policy on the maintenance of power of two authoritarian states.

China under Mao Zedong, 1949–76

Mao Zedong held authoritarian control over the **People's Republic of China (PRC)** from 1949 until his death in 1976. A revolutionary, military leader and **ideologue**, his historical reputation has divided many. There is no doubt though that he had a transformative effect on the history of China.

Mao's rise to power

Revised

On 1 October 1949, Mao proclaimed the beginning of the PRC in Beijing when the **Chinese Communist Party (CCP)** took control of the country. This section considers the years leading up to this point.

■ Conditions in which states emerged

Throughout the years leading up to 1949 China suffered from many economic problems. For most Chinese people, life was tough and conditions were harsh.

■ Long-term economic problems
- China had failed to modernize successfully during the nineteenth century and large numbers people were living in poverty, roughly 80% of the population at the start of the twentieth century.
- The nineteenth century also saw defeat in wars (for example, the **Opium Wars** and the **First Sino-Japanese War**), which had weakened China economically.
- European empires had successfully imposed unequal treaties on China.

■ Economic conditions in the early twentieth century
- After the 1911 revolution, the Chinese economic system did not improve significantly.
- The **warlord era** saw the weakening of China as the country became fragmented and divided.
- During the **Nanjing Decade**, **Chiang Kai-shek** (Jang Jieshi), the leader of the **Guomindang (GMD)** – also called the Nationalists – introduced some economic reforms including the building of roads and railways. This led to modest economic improvements.
- China's economy was devastated by the impact of war, first the war with Japan from 1937 to 1945 and later the **Chinese Civil War** between 1946 and 1949.
- Hyperinflation was a major problem during both the **Second Sino-Japanese War** and the Chinese Civil War, making conditions very difficult for people across China (see Sources 1 and 2 opposite).

THE IMPACT OF HYPERINFLATION

During the Chinese Civil War, hyperinflation had a severe impact on China's economy. Examine the source material to gain more depth on how this economic condition aided the CCP in their rise to power.

SOURCE 1

Extract from R. Keith Schoppa, *Twentieth Century China: A History in Documents*, Oxford University Press, New York, 2011, pages 115–16. A. Doak Barnett was an American living in Shanghai in 1947 and he described the economic conditions in Shanghai at that time.

One cannot escape the inflation in Shanghai, any more than one can elsewhere in China. It is ever present and all important. A dollar is worth more today than it will be tomorrow; consequently all money is 'hot money'. As a general rule, people spend money as soon as they get it, if they can … The manager of one of Shanghai's large private banks reports that the US dollar value of savings deposits in his bank has been reduced from $20 million to $100,000. Insurance savings have been wiped out completely. A Chinese friend of mine, whose insurance policy was worth roughly US$1000 before the war, estimates that it is now worth US $00.0064, less than a penny!

1 What does Source 1 tell you about the economic conditions in China during the civil war?

2 How would the economic conditions affect people across China and make the conditions for the CCP to take power more favourable?

SOURCE 2

Extract from 'China's Great Inflation Helped Bring the Communists to Power' by Richard Ebeling, from thedailybell.com (available at www.thedailybell.com/editorials/richard-ebeling-chinas-great-inflation-helped-bring-the-communists-to-power/).

It would be an exaggeration to say that China's Great Inflation was the only cause for the defeat of the Nationalist government and the victory of the Chinese communists. The Nationalist Party was dictatorial in its structure, notorious for its corruption and abuse of political power and often as ruthless as the communists in its use of military force.

But it is nonetheless true that whatever basis of popular support Chiang's government might have had against the communists at the end of the Second World War, especially among the country's middle class, was undermined by the inflation. It destroyed the wealth and savings of the Chinese middle class and created chaos in virtually all commercial dealings due to the loss of a reliable and stable medium of exchange for purposes of rational economic calculation and business planning.

In addition, the inflation and its effects drove some segments of the rural population into a more severe poverty than even the war had generated. Thus, whatever support the Nationalist government may have had in the countryside soon withered away, as well.

3 What does Source 2 suggest about the importance of hyperinflation for the rise to power of the CCP?

4 Do you agree with the perspective in Source 2? Can you think of any limitations?

4 China under Mao Zedong, 1949–76

■ Social division
- China had high levels of social inequality leading up to the Chinese Civil War.
- Large numbers of agricultural workers lived in poverty with a basic standard of living.
- The warlord era highlights the regional divisions within China; even after 1927 many areas remained outside Nationalist control.
- Wealth tended to be focused in urban areas, for example Shanghai was very prosperous during the Nanjing Decade.
- Increasingly, people were unhappy with Chiang and the GMD and saw the CCP as an alternative.

■ Weakness of political system
- The **Xinhai revolution** failed to establish a strong system of governance after 1912.
- The early Republic of China under **Yuan Shikai** only lasted for a few years. While in power, Yuan increasingly used dictatorial methods prior to his death in 1916, at one point declaring himself emperor of a new dynasty.
- China's political system was further weakened during the warlord era.
- The GMD's ideology was based on the teachings of **Sun Yat-sen** (Sun Yixian), which offered some promise of improvements for Chinese people. His ideology included the **Three Principles of the People** (democracy, nationalism and people's livelihood) but Chiang's commitment to these principles was limited.
- The Nanjing Decade did bring some stability, but the GMD was unpopular with the poorer sections of society. It had also failed to consolidate its control over the whole of China and needed to make strategic alliances with warlords.
- The political system introduced by Chiang and the Nationalists was conservative and authoritarian. Many of Chiang's ideas were ineffective, for example the **New Life Movement** introduced during the 1930s failed in its objectives to bring about cultural change.

■ Impact of war
- China lost the First Sino-Japanese War in 1895 and tension continued between the two countries in the subsequent years. This included the **21 Demands** made by Japan during the First World War, the disagreements over the return of Shandong Province in 1919, and the Japanese invasion of Manchuria in 1931.
- The Second Sino-Japanese War, 1937–45, devastated China through loss of human life and economic damage; it also weakened the GMD's control. Chinese people felt outraged at many of the atrocities committed during the war, especially the Nanjing Massacre in 1937.
- Around 20 million Chinese people lost their lives between 1937 and 1945 in the war against Japan. The dead included around 17 million civilians.
- The Chinese Civil War broke out in 1946; this created the conditions for the CCP to take control of the whole of China. The GMD had been significantly weakened by the years of fighting Japan and Chiang's authority and popularity had declined as a result of war.

Mao's rise to power

CONDITIONS THAT LED TO THE RISE TO POWER OF MAO

Create a mind map to highlight the different conditions that led to the rise to power of Mao. Use the information provided and any additional knowledge you would like to include. You should aim to include information on economic conditions, social division, weakness of the political system and the impact of war.

EXPLAIN THE SIGNIFICANCE

One of the history concepts is significance. Use the table below to reflect on the significance of the different conditions affecting China prior to 1949 in relation to the rise to power of Mao and the CCP.

Conditions in China prior to 1949	How would this event help Mao and the CCP to take control of China?
High levels of poverty in China, especially in rural areas	
Economic hardship during the wars, hyperinflation crisis from 1937 onwards	
Unpopularity of Chiang Kai-shek and the GMD, failure to implement the Three Principles of the People	
Impact of the war with Japan on China	

4 China under Mao Zedong, 1949–76

■ Methods used to establish authoritarian states

The CCP was formed in July 1921 in Shanghai. Founding members included **Li Dazhao**, **Chen Duxiu** and Mao Zedong. The **New Culture Movement**, the **May 4th Movement** and the success of the Bolshevik Revolution all contributed to this ideological development.

■ Ideology
- Ideology was important to the CCP's rise to power. The party initially followed Marxism–Leninism.
- The Soviet Union set up Comintern to spread communism worldwide. In the 1920s this had an influence on the early development of the CCP.
- Gradually, a challenge to the Soviet ideological position emerged, mainly through Mao's ideas and teachings. Mao spoke regularly about the revolutionary potential of agricultural labourers in China who made up the majority of the population. He believed that they could carry out the revolution, as opposed to the Soviet ideology that stressed that revolution would come from industrial workers.
- Mao's ideology is reflected in the saying 'The peasants are the sea; we are the fish. We live in the sea.'
- The CCP held ideological appeal through policies such as land reform and gender equality. It was also seen to be committed to nationalism, which was popular with people during the time when Japan was at war with China.
- Between 1935 and 1949, the CCP, now led by Mao, was based in **Yanan** (Yan'an). In this location it was able to develop ideology and policies.

■ The role of leaders
- Mao Zedong played an important role in the CCP from the outset. He had studied Marxism while at university in Beijing and he adapted the ideology to suit the needs of China as he saw it.
- Mao was also a military leader; he led the **Autumn Harvest Uprising** in September 1927.
- Mao made use of **guerrilla warfare** tactics and continued this approach to military engagements throughout the 1930s and 1940s. He wrote *On Guerrilla Warfare* in 1937 on these different tactics.
- The **Long March** of 1934–5 was an important series of events for the CCP. The communists managed to survive, but lost many of their members. Mao was also able to use the Long March to increase his position and power within the CCP.
- There were many other CCP members who played influential roles, including **Zhou Enlai** and **Liu Shaoqi**.
- Some of the CCP leadership disagreed with Mao's ideology and took a more pro-Soviet view; the **28 Bolsheviks** who had been trained in Moscow were especially critical.
- Mao launched a number of self-criticism campaigns during the early 1940s such as the **Rectification of Conduct Campaign**. He wanted to remove any revisionist ideas from the CCP. He taught **revolutionary correctness** to keep his followers strictly in line with his ideological position.

■ Persuasion and coercion
- The CCP had very different policies and approaches from the GMD. Throughout its control of the **Jiangxi Soviet**, and later the Yanan years, it was able to increase membership through the popularity of its policies.
- The CCP particularly appealed to the rural peasantry with policies such as land reform, literacy campaigns and medical programmes, and the creation of local peasant associations to provide representation and the ending of **usury** (a system which placed high levels of interest on loans).
- Peasant membership of the party grew from 40,000 in 1937 to 1 million in 1945.
- Rules were established for good conduct by the **Red Army**, such as 'be courteous and help out where you can' and 'replace all damaged articles'.
- Coercion was also a tactic and there was a threat of force from the CCP if people did not cooperate with its practices. The communists could also veto the local peasant associations if they did not agree with their decisions.

Mao's rise to power

COMPARING STUDENT RESPONSES

Review the following extracts of student responses to an essay question on the rise to power of Mao. Each paragraph is written about the same topic: the role of ideology.

Student 1

Further to this, the ideology of Mao and the CCP contributed to their victory and emergence of an authoritarians state. Mao's ideology was based on not only Marxism but also his own personal adaptation for the conditions in China. Recognizing that the vast proportion of Chinese people were agricultural labourers, he suggested that they had revolutionary potential to transform China. This differed to the versions of communism adhered to by the Soviet Union who saw the industrial workers as the group capable of carrying out revolution. Mao's focus on the role of agricultural labourers may have increased his popularity, as a wide range of policies was targeted to bring them a better standard of living, such as land redistribution.

Good use of a connective. Connectives are very effective for linking written answers together. See page 13 for an activity on this.

Use of a comparison point. It is good practice to use comparative language in your Paper 2 essays. This shows that you have a clear historical awareness.

Student 2

The ideology of the communists helped them gain power. They passed policies such as land reform and gave more equal status to women. When Mao was based in Yanan, he carried out different policies and the CCP grew in popularity with an increased membership. Mao's Long March was also important to his power.

The Long March occurred in 1934 and involved the CCP retreating across China. During the march, many people died and the conditions were terrible.

The student explains the ideas well and provides an evaluative point.

Relevant examples are provided but does the student explain in enough detail? A missed opportunity to develop the response.

Is the answer now losing focus on ideology?

After reviewing these responses, try writing a couple of paragraphs on the role of ideology in the rise to power of Mao. When you have completed your writing, annotate your text with positive comments and areas for improvement.

FURTHER PRACTICE QUESTIONS

The following questions can also help you to revise for the rise to power of Mao in China. The first question is focused on conditions and the second question is focused on methods. Write an essay plan and then have a go at the questions.

Examine the role played by social division and the impact of war for the rise to power of one authoritarian ruler.

'The emergence of Mao as ruler of China was due to his leadership and ideology.' To what extent do you agree with this statement?

63

The use of force

- Early examples of CCP violence against opposition can be seen in the **Futian Incident** in 1930 where hundreds of Red Army members were executed, most likely under Mao's orders.
- Mao's ideology indicated an acceptance and willingness for the use of force where necessary.
- Land redistribution was often done by force, where landlords had their land confiscated from them; this often involved violence and a loss of life.

> **SOURCE 3**
>
> Extract from Mao Zedong, *Selected Works of Mao Tse-tung*, Vol. II, Foreign Languages Press, Beijing, 1965, pages 224–5 (available at www.marxists.org/reference/archive/mao/works/red-book/ch05.htm).
>
> Experience in the class struggle in the era of imperialism teaches us that it is only by the power of the gun that the working class and the labouring masses can defeat the armed bourgeoisie and landlords; in this sense we may say that only with guns can the whole world be transformed. We are advocates of the abolition of war, we do not want war; but war can only be abolished through war, and in order to get rid of the gun it is necessary to take up the gun.

Propaganda

- The Long March was used as propaganda by the CCP, giving Mao and other leaders cult status.
- Mao's cult of personality grew as his writings and image were promoted by the CCP.
- The rules of conduct of the Red Army were a form of propaganda as they worked as self-promotion.
- The leaders wrote literature to promote the movement, for example Liu Shaoqi wrote *How to Be a Good Communist* in 1939.

The Chinese Civil War, 1945–9

After Japan had been defeated in 1945, a civil war began between the CCP and the GMD. A conference at Chongqing was held in 1945 between the warring parties with the USA acting as mediator. It failed to deliver lasting peace between the two parties. Despite early successes during the civil war, the GMD lost successive campaigns and eventually retreated to Taiwan in 1949.

The following table is a summary of the relative weaknesses of the GMD against the strengths of the CCP.

GMD weaknesses	CCP strengths
- Poor training and military strategy by GMD. Chiang used similar tactics to what he had always used and failed to deal effectively with guerrilla warfare from CCP - Low morale among troops, especially after years of fighting Japan - Growing unpopularity of Chiang as leader of the country - Poor economy during the war with high levels of inflation made conditions for ordinary Chinese people much worse. Merchant and business owners were badly affected - Repressive policies by GMD made them unpopular with people across the country, especially when compared with the ideological appeal of the CCP	- Mao's careful strategy to defend territory early on in the war before taking on an attacking strategy. Success of different campaigns, for example Manchuria, capture of Beijing during **Pingjin Campaign** towards the end of the war - Military strategy and tactics of Mao, use of guerrilla warfare tactics. Red Army's resourcefulness and code of conduct - Growing popularity of the CCP. It was able to mobilize large numbers of agricultural labourers to help with its campaigns during the war

CONDITIONS OR METHODS?

Read through the events that are important for understanding Mao's rise to power and tick whether you view them as conditions or methods.

Event	Conditions?	Methods?
Land reform in Jiangxi Province		
Guerrilla warfare tactics		
Hyperinflation in China during the 1940s		
The New Culture Movement		
Mao's adaptation of Marxism–Leninism		
High levels of poverty in China, majority of population were agricultural labourers		
Code of Conduct for the Red Army		
Growing unpopularity of GMD leadership		
Mao's military strategy during the civil war		
Rectification campaigns		
Treatment of landlords by the CCP		
Failure of early Chinese Republic and the warlord era		

PROPAGANDA AND THE ROLE OF MAO

SOURCE 4

'The Long March', a poem by Mao Zedong from September 1935, quoted in David L. Weitzman, *Mao Tse-tung and The Chinese Revolution*, Foreign Languages Press, Beijing, 1953 (available at http://afe.easia.columbia.edu/special/china_1900_mao_march.htm).

The Red Army fears not the trials of the Long March
And thinks nothing of a thousand mountains and rivers.
The Wuling Ridges spread out like ripples;
The Wumeng Ranges roll like balls of clay.
Warmly are the cliffs wrapped in clouds washed by the Gold Sand;
Chilly are the iron chains lying across the width of the Great Ferry.
A thousand acres of snow on the Min Mountain delight
My troops who have just left them behind.

5. Mao wrote the poem in Source 4 about the Long March in 1935. How do you think works like this would have been used as propaganda for the CCP?

SOURCE 5

Chairman Mao (left) speaking to agricultural labourers of Yangchialing in Yunan, Northern Shensi Province, during the Second Sino-Japanese War, 1937–45.

6. How do images like this one help us to understand the reasons why Mao and the CCP were able to take control of China?

4 China under Mao Zedong, 1949–76

Mao's consolidation and maintenance of power

Revised

After winning the civil war, Mao and the CCP began the process of consolidating control over China.

Methods for the consolidation and maintenance of power

Legal methods
- The country was divided into six regions, each controlled by a chairman, party secretary, military commander and political commissar.
- The **People's Liberation Army (PLA)** played an influential role in the political control of China.
- The PRC was a one-party state and although party officials were elected, they could only be party members.
- The Politburo ran China at a national level.
- From 1950 onwards, a series of **Reunification Campaigns** were set up to consolidate China's borders as well as weaken any independence movements. These included taking control of Tibet and Xinjiang Province in the west, as well as Guangdong province in the south.
- The CCP introduced a variety of legal forms, including the 1954 constitution.

Use of force
- The CCP carried out a number of measures to consolidate its control over the population of China, specifically targeting different groups in different campaigns.
- The **Anti-Campaigns** were set up to remove from China any people who were seen to be against the CCP's interests. This especially included people who had been wealthy prior to its takeover of China.
- People's rights could be limited if they were suspected of being against the interests of the party, making it difficult to gain work and housing.
- Landlords were a particularly vilified group. Many landlords were put on public trial and humiliated. **Speak Bitterness** meetings encouraged public grievances to be heard against the landlords. Numbers vary, but recent estimates suggest that around 1 million landlords may have been killed by the early 1950s.
- The Three and Five Anti-Campaigns were launched in 1951 and 1952, respectively, targeting different forms of corruption that were seen to be a problem at the time. For example, the Three Anti-Campaign focused on corruption, waste and bureaucracy.
- Policies encouraged spying on neighbours, which created an atmosphere of fear.
- In the early consolidation phase, religious groups were also targeted with the closing down of places of worship and the denunciation of religions such as Christianity and Buddhism.
- Gangsters and members of organized crime groups were also targeted by the CCP.
- A network of prison camps, the *laogai*, were set up across China. They were designed to 're-educate' people. They became a source of labour during the economic projects of the Great Leap Forward – basically slave labour. They were located in harsh areas, where the climate was brutal and disease spread easily in the camps. Millions of people were held in the camps during Mao's rule over China.

Case study: the Hundred Flowers and Anti-Rightist Campaigns
- In 1957, Mao encouraged open criticism of the party, stating 'Let a hundred flowers bloom; let a hundred schools of thought contend.'
- This encouraged people to speak out and criticize different things about how the CCP ruled China and also included **denunciations** of officials. Some people also criticized Mao himself.
- Mao saw these critics as examples of 'rightists' and **capitalist roaders**. He ordered a crackdown on those who were critical, arresting and imprisoning many people. This was known as the **Anti-Rightist Campaign**.
- Historians differ in their interpretations of the Hundred Flowers Campaign. Some say that it was an intentional ruse to remove opposition, while others suggest that there was an original motive to allow ideas and criticism to be expressed and the crackdown had not been planned.

Use of propaganda
- The CCP made extensive use of propaganda and censorship.
- This included posters promoting different policies, often using socialist realism techniques.
- The arts were censored (especially during the Cultural Revolution, see page 72) and any works commissioned were to support CCP ideology.
- Loudspeakers were widely used to spread the message of the CCP.

- The cult of personality of Mao was very important. For example, in 1966 his swim in the Yangtze River was used to promote his position as a strong leader and the **Little Red Book** was distributed throughout the country.
- Censorship involved removing 'revisionist' lines of thought or those which painted the West in a positive light.

Charismatic leadership

- The leadership of Mao was important to the consolidation and maintenance of the CCP's control of China. Mao was a figurehead for the party.
- Mao's image was seen throughout China, and his speeches, writings and teachings were promoted.
- Even when Mao was connected to the disaster of the **Great Leap Forward** (see page 70) and the subsequent famine, he was not heavily criticized.
- Mao's authority was promoted by the **Gang of Four** during the **Cultural Revolution**.

COMPLETE THIS PARAGRAPH

Fill in the paragraph below to practise your writing on the CCP's use of force in its consolidation of power.

> A variety of groups were targeted during the early years of the People's Republic of China ...

REFLECTING ON SIGNIFICANCE

7. How significant do you think the following were in the CCP's consolidation of power?
   a) Establishing political control, party structures and national borders. b) Mass campaigns and the anti-movements. c) The Hundred Flowers and Anti-Rightist Campaigns.

PROPAGANDA TECHNIQUES

- Go to the website www.chineseposters.net and then search for the section called 'Building the People's Republic of China'.
- Examine the different messages and techniques used in the different posters so that you can use a couple as examples.
- When writing about the use of propaganda, providing a specific example is a good way to demonstrate your knowledge and understanding.

CREATE AN ESSAY PLAN

Create an essay plan for the following question:

To what extent was force the defining factor that allowed Mao to consolidate and maintain power over China?

The following steps can help you in your planning:

- Write out the question and check the command term. Are there any terms that need defining?
- What are your initial thoughts about what you need to include in your response?
- What will be your main points for structuring your response?
- What evidence will help you to answer the question effectively? Remember to link the relevant evidence to the different main points.
- What perspectives can be used? For example, different interpretations of the Hundred Flowers Campaign.

Foreign policy under Mao, 1949–76

Foreign policy under Mao involved a difficult and changing relationship with both the Soviet Union and the USA. The PRC was also involved in a number of conflicts and international disputes under Mao, generally located within close proximity to China's borders.

China and the Soviet Union

- Mao and Stalin had differences of opinion on ideology. Stalin rejected Mao's interpretation of Marxism based on Chinese conditions.
- In the early days of the PRC, the CCP needed help from Stalin and the Soviet Union in its consolidation of power.
- Mao visited Moscow in 1950, resulting in the **Sino-Soviet Treaty of Friendship, Alliance and Mutual Assistance**. The treaty involved loans from the Soviet Union to China (with high interest rates) and the deployment of thousands of Soviet 'advisers' to China.
- The CCP depended strongly on Soviet aid through the 1950s and the USSR was involved in the economic planning in the first Five-Year Plan.
- The **Korean War** of 1950–3 placed a strain on Sino-Soviet relations as Mao felt that China made greater sacrifices in the support of North Korea than had the Soviet Union. However, China's successful military encounters during the war bolstered Mao's position in China and internationally.
- Sino-Soviet relations worsened after the death of Stalin in 1953. **Nikita Khrushchev**'s **Secret Speech** (which involved criticism of Stalin) in 1956 was badly received by Mao. Mao also disliked the new Soviet policy of **peaceful coexistence** with the West.
- Mao frequently described Khrushchev negatively, as a 'Soviet revisionist', and placed himself as the ideological leader of world communism.
- China had invested heavily in nuclear arms since the early 1950s and this was a source of tension. In 1964, the PRC had achieved nuclear capability, bolstering Mao's authority in China and in the developing world.
- Relationships did not improve with the appointment of new Soviet leader **Leonid Brezhnev** in the late 1960s.
- In 1969, border skirmishes led to military conflict between the two countries, the lowest point in the Sino-Soviet split.

China and the USA

- Relationships between the USA and China were poor after 1949. American policy-makers felt that they had 'lost China', as they had invested heavily in Chiang's Nationalists and were unhappy with the result of the civil war.
- The USA recognized Taiwan as the home of the official government of China and not the PRC. This caused major diplomatic tensions.
- Anti-US propaganda was commonly used in the PRC, often describing Americans as imperialists.
- The USA and China fought a **proxy war** in Korea, significantly increasing tension between the two nations.
- The USA sided with Taiwan in any dispute with the PRC. The first **Taiwan Straits Crisis** in 1955 nearly brought nuclear confrontation to the region.
- Relationships continued to be poor into the 1960s, as a result of China's acquisition of nuclear weapons and the **Vietnam War**.
- By the early 1970s, relations between the two nations started to improve. An important step was the recognition of the PRC at the United Nations in 1971, although the USA did not initially support its membership.
- US President **Richard Nixon** visited Mao in 1972. This led to improved relations – sometimes called the **Sino-American Rapprochement** – leading, later, to increased economic interdependence between the nations.

REFLECTING ON FOREIGN POLICY

- Step 1. Use the table below as a template to reflect on how each foreign policy event would affect Mao's consolidation and/or maintenance of power.

Foreign policy event	How do you think it would affect Mao's position?
Creation of the PRC and the establishment of its borders	
The Korean War	
Development of nuclear weapons	
Sino-Soviet Treaty of Friendship	
Poor relations with the USA in the 1950s	
Mao's rivalries with Khrushchev	
Sino-Soviet split	
Recognition at United Nations	
Sino-American Rapprochement	

- Step 2. Now create a diamond nine to rank the importance of the different foreign policy events to the consolidation and maintenance of power.
- Consider which events you would want to discuss in an essay question.

- Step 3. Consider the following essay question.

Examine the importance of foreign policy towards the consolidation and maintenance of authoritarian states.

- Take a look at this essay question and then consider the following questions:
  a What is the question asking you to do? Will you need to discuss more than one authoritarian state?
  b What is the command term? How will that affect the structure of your essay?
  c When writing about Mao and the PRC, what evidence would you use to explain the importance of foreign policy? Refer to steps 1 and 2 here.
  d Is there scope to discuss the limitations of foreign policy and importance of other factors?
  e What other authoritarian state(s) would you choose to write about? Is there the option to make historical comparisons?

4 China under Mao Zedong, 1949–76

Mao's domestic policies: aims and results

Economic policies

The first Five-Year Plan

- Mao used the economic model of the **Five-Year Plan** to restructure the Chinese economy. This was under the influence of the Soviet Union.
- The first Five-Year Plan was introduced in 1953. The main focus was on the development of heavy industry. Soviet advisers and experts worked in China to help carry out the plan.
- Steel production had reached 5.35 million tons in 1957; coal production had also increased significantly.
- Agriculture did not improve as much as industrial developments during the first Five-Year Plan; grain output declined. Cooperatives were set up, where groups of farmers joined together; however, these were replaced by larger communes in the second Five-Year Plan.
- Major engineering works were carried out, including the building of major road and rail bridges.
- The Soviet Union charged interest on the loans to China during the first Five-Year Plan, placing a strain on the Sino-Soviet relationship.
- Overall, the first Five-Year Plan was successful in developing heavy industry. It also aided the CCP's consolidation of control over China, with higher levels of state ownership.

The second Five-Year Plan

- Mao launched the second Five-Year Plan in 1958; it is also known as the Great Leap Forward.
- The overall aim was to try and catch up with Western industrialized nations in a short space of time. Mao also wanted to reduce China's reliance on the Soviet Union.
- The Great Leap Forward included a variety of targets, including significant increases in steel and food production.
- **Backyard steel furnaces** were set up all over China as the masses worked to reach the targets. These furnaces often produced poor-quality metal that was essentially useless.
- Large **communes** were set up during this time in a process called collectivization; there were thousands of communes across China.
- Communes took the ownership of land away from agricultural labourers; all **surplus** produce became state owned.
- This led to a severe disruption of the usual agricultural practices, resulting in a decrease in food production.
- Propaganda was used to promote collectivization and the policies of the Great Leap Forward, often hiding the reality that people were starving from a lack of food.
- Meat production decreased from 4.3 million tons in 1958 to 1.3 million tons in 1960.
- A severe famine occurred between 1959 and 1961, killing approximately 40 million people. CCP officials blamed poor weather.

Diminished power?

- After the disastrous Great Leap Forward, there was an opportunity for members of the CCP to criticize Mao's failings as leader.
- The major criticism came from **Peng Dehuai** at the **Lushan Conference** in 1959. Peng was the defence minister and he described the suffering of the people as a result of the famine.
- Peng was alone in his criticism and this resulted in him being isolated and losing his political power.
- Mao took a step back after the Great Leap Forward, and two moderate CCP party members, **Deng Xiaoping** and Liu Shaoqi, took on the role of helping China to recover from the famine.

SOURCE 6

'The commune is like a giant dragon, production is visibly awe inspiring': a Chinese poster from 1959.

Mao's domestic policies: aims and results

THE CONSEQUENCES OF THE GREAT LEAP FORWARD

- The Great Leap Forward is now widely acknowledged to be an absolute disaster both in terms of economic progress and in terms of human loss of life and suffering.
- Use the following sources to develop your understanding and collect evidence.

SOURCE 7

'Four pests', quoted in Geoff Stewart, *China 1900–76*, Heinemann, Oxford, 2006, pages 117–18.

Mao announced the extermination of the Four Pests. It led to the Four No's campaign: no rats, no sparrows, no flies and no mosquitoes. The impact on rats was not notable, but the sparrows died in their millions. Mao had decided that they ate the grain and food production would be boosted if sparrows were no more … Cart loads of dead and dying birds were to be seen. Here was mass mobilisation at work. When a plague of caterpillars emerged in 1958 attacking plants and crops, sparrows were dropped from the death list – sparrows eat caterpillars.

SOURCE 8

'Unrealistic production targets', quoted in Jung Chang and Jon Halliday, *Mao: The Unknown Story*, Vintage Books, London, 2007, page 449.

When he boasted to Communist leaders in Moscow in 1957 that 'China would overtake Britain in fifteen years' (which he later shortened to three) and when he told the Chinese he was fully confident that China could 'overtake' America in ten years, steel output was what he had in mind. Mao set the 1958 target at 10.7 million tons. How this came about illustrates his broadbrush approach to economics. Sitting by his swimming pool in Zhonnanhai on 19th June he said to the metallurgy minister: 'Last year, steel output was 5.3 million tons. Can you double it this year?' The yes-man said: 'All right.' And that was that.

SOURCE 9

'Famine', quoted in Michael Lynch, *The People's Republic of China Since 1949*, Hodder & Stoughton, London, 1998, page 31.

It was certainly the case that millions died in the countryside. Hunger was not unknown in the urban areas but it was in the rural provinces of China that the famine was at its worst. Henan and Anhui were particularly badly affected. Gansu, Sichuan, Hebei and Xinjiang were other areas that experienced appalling suffering. Parents sold their children and husbands sold their wives for food. Women prostituted themselves to obtain food for their families, and there were many instances of peasants offering themselves as slaves to anyone who would feed them.

Source extract	What evidence does the source provide about the problems during the Great Leap Forward?	How could you use this evidence when writing about the impact of the Great Leap Forward?
Four pests		
Unrealistic production targets		
Famine		

REFLECTING ON ECONOMIC POLICY

How might the economic policies of Mao help or hinder his consolidation and maintenance of power? (Refer to the first and second Five-Year Plans.)

Help?	Hinder?

Mao's cultural policies

Aims
Mao wanted to reshape Chinese culture through his ideological belief in revolution. **Individualism** was discouraged and the interests of the collective and the state were to be supported by culture. **Proletarian** art and culture was encouraged and social realism was used to promote these aims.

The Cultural Revolution, 1966–76 (approximately)
The Cultural Revolution was Mao's method to re-establish absolute control over China after the Great Leap Forward. Historical debate centres on how much control Mao had over the Cultural Revolution and whether it was, in fact, driven by the Gang of Four:

- The Cultural Revolution began in the mid-1960s. Its spark was a reaction to the play *The Dismissal of Hai Rui from Office*. Criticised by **Yao Wenyuan**, the play was seen to be too similar to the conflict between Mao and Peng Dehuai during the Great Leap Forward. This provided an excuse for the Cultural Revolution.
- Mao and the Gang of Four set out to remove any 'revisionists' and 'capitalist roaders' within the party.
- People were encouraged to attack the 'four olds': old thoughts, old habits, old culture and old customs. Mao's authority was promoted by widespread reading of his Little Red Book of quotations.
- Young people were particularly enthusiastic about their role in the Cultural Revolution. The **Red Guard** was set up to cause chaos during the Cultural Revolution and to physically attack revisionism and the 'four olds'.
- An important moment during the Cultural Revolution was the removal of Liu Shaoqi and Deng Xiaoping from their positions of power. They were accused of 'revisionism'. Liu eventually died as a result of his treatment during the Cultural Revolution. Deng was exiled, but managed to survive.

Mass campaigns during the Cultural Revolution
- The Red Guard was called to order after the first few years of the Cultural Revolution as its members were becoming increasingly out of control.
- The 'up to the mountains and down to the villages' campaign involved young, urban Chinese people living among agricultural labourers in rural areas.
- The 'cleansing the class ranks' campaign launched by Jiang Qing was a series of violent purges of anyone seen to be capitalist. Thousands were killed and injured across China.

Ending the Cultural Revolution
- By the 1970s the Cultural Revolution was losing its momentum.
- The death of Lin Biao in a mysterious plane crash led to questions about the leadership of the CCP.
- Gradually, moderates such as Zhou Enlai (and later Deng Xiaoping) became more influential and radicals such as the Gang of Four saw their power diminish.
- The death of Mao in 1976 was the end of the Cultural Revolution. In the following years, a power struggle occurred that would see Deng Xiaoping succeed, and the Gang of Four put to trial and imprisoned for their actions during the Cultural Revolution.

THE AIMS AND RESULTS OF MAO'S DOMESTIC POLICIES

- Step 1. Spend some time clarifying your understanding of the aims and results of Mao's domestic policies by completing the table below.

Social	Economic
Aims	Aims
• Removal of opposition/mass campaigns • Repression of religion • Improved conditions for women • Recognition of minorities/weaken separatist groups and traditions	• Mass economic development of China • Reduce dependency on the Soviet Union • Catch up with West • Policies of collectivization and industrialization
Results?	Results?
Cultural	**Political**
Aims	Aims
• Controlling the arts through ideology • Removing traditions such as the 'four olds' • Strengthening Mao's cult of personality • Censorship and propaganda to control society	• Establishing legal systems, for example the 1954 constitution • Securing borders and creating the political structure of the PRC • Seeking and removing opposition, for example the Hundred Flowers Movement • Continuous revolution through the Cultural Revolution
Results?	Results?

- Step 2. Now reflect on this question: In what ways had Mao achieved authoritarian control in China? Think about the ways you could use the following as evidence in a response to this question:
    - Hundred Flowers Campaign
    - repression of religion
    - Five-Year Plans
    - Great Leap Forward and famine
    - propaganda
    - mass campaigns
    - prison camps
    - treatment of opposition.

4 China under Mao Zedong, 1949–76

■ Mao's social policies

■ Religion
- Karl Marx famously said that 'religion is the opium of the people'. Not surprisingly, as in other communist dictatorships, religious groups experienced difficulties under Mao's rule.
- After 1949, religious practice was banned in China, with many religious figures targeted for abuse. The CCP feared that people could challenge its authority through religion and religious organizations, especially in remote areas of China where many people followed Buddhism and Islam.
- Propaganda was used to reinforce the anti-religious message.
- Peasant folk traditions were also discouraged, including songs and folk stories.
- New routines and rituals were introduced which celebrated the benefits of communism.
- Some churches were allowed to stay open under direct state control; they were known as the **Patriotic Churches**.
- Religion and traditions, including **Confucianism**, were particularly targeted during the Cultural Revolution.

■ Minorities
- The **Han** are the dominant ethnic group in China, with at least 80% of the population.
- Fifty-four minority groups in China were officially recognized by 1957 by the CCP.
- Propaganda posters promoted unity and recognition of minority groups in China and they were often presented in stereotypical ethnic clothing, usually singing and dancing.
- **Xinjiang Province** in north-west China is made up of a number of various minority Chinese groups including the **Uighur, Hui and Kirghiz** people, and these groups had less loyalty to Beijing. The CCP feared that they could stir up religious and nationalist opposition to their authority.
- The government introduced the process of settling Han Chinese people into Xinjiang and Tibet to weaken this potential challenge.

■ Women and the family
- China was traditionally a **patriarchal** society.
- The CCP advocated gender equality.
- The CCP passed the **Marriage Law** in 1950 (see Source 11 opposite).
- Women were able to own and sell land as a result of the land redistribution policies of the early 1950s, although this was undermined with the creation of communes during collectivization.
- The number of women in the workforce quadrupled from 8% to 32% between 1949 and 1976.
- Rural and religious areas had less success with regard to gender equality, with female infants considered less important or valuable than male infants.
- There were limited numbers of women in political office, although the number of women in the National People's Congress rose from 14% to 23% between 1954 and 1975.
- The communes skewed family roles, with the family unit often separated into different living quarters.
- During the Cultural Revolution, the family came under further attack, with the love for parents being replaced with the love for Mao and the CCP. Young people were often instructed to denounce their parents or extended family if they were seen to be against the movement.

SOURCE INVESTIGATION

- Read Source 10. In what ways do you think the lives of women improved as a result of the 1950 Marriage Law?

SOURCE 10

Extract from 'The Marriage Law of the Peoples Republic of China', 1950, in R. Keith Schoppa, *Twentieth Century China: A History in Documents*, Oxford University Press, New York, 2011, pages 134–5.

Article 1: The feudal marriage system based on arbitrary and compulsory arrangements, and the supremacy of men over women is abolished.

Article 2: Bigamy, concubinage, child betrothal, interference in the re-marriage of widows and the exaction [payment] of money or gifts in connection with marriage shall be prohibited.

Article 3: Marriage shall be based on the complete willingness of the two parties. No third party shall be allowed to interfere …

Article 17: Divorce shall be granted when husband and wife both desire it.

- Read Source 11. What does this source suggest about the reality of life for many women living in China during this time?

SOURCE 11

Extract from Fox Butterfield, *China: Alive in the Bitter Sea*, Bantam Books, New York, 1990, page 166.

Lihua recalled that in her village, girls were not sent to school at all, for their parents still regard them as 'outsiders'. At marriage, they will move away. Girl babies in her village are called 'a thousand ounces of gold', boys were called 'a million ounces of gold'.

In the commune, women are usually given the most back-breaking labour, transplanting rice or picking beans, while their men folk are off driving tractors or acting as cadres. An American sociologist who lived on a commune in Hebei province calculated that women actually did 80 percent of all the field work.

- Examine Source 12. Why would the symbolism of female parachutists help to promote CCP ideology and the role of women in society?

SOURCE 12

A propaganda poster promoting women's new freedoms in China as a result of the CCP policies, 1955.

Exam focus

Guidance and sample question and answers

Read the essay question below.

Compare and contrast the effects of social policies on women in two authoritarian states.

■ Demands of the question

- Compare and contrast questions can be asked on the Authoritarian states section of the IB history exam.
- Of particular importance is referring to both states throughout your answer.
- This means that, ideally, you should aim to write a running commentary on similarities and differences of the two case studies *together* rather than discuss each individually.
- Venn diagrams can be very useful when planning compare and contrast questions.
- Choose two authoritarian states and then have a go at drawing a Venn diagram (see the example diagram below) on the social policies affecting women.
- This will help you to plan an essay. The evidence that goes in the middle should be the similarities.
- Read through the two extracts from answers to the same essay question.
- Read the teacher annotations and comments.
- What do you think of the responses?
- Identify the positives from the essays and identify things you would do differently.

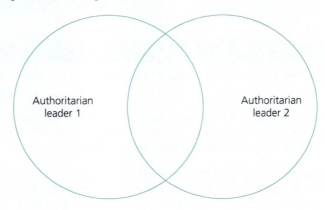

The People's Republic of China (PRC) under Mao Zedong and the Soviet Union under Joseph Stalin were two authoritarian states that carried out a range of social policies that affected the people living there. In both states, the status and treatment of women provides an insight into the ideological beliefs of the two leaders. At first we can see a range of similarities in the treatment of women, which included providing greater rights both within the home and in the workplace. However, when examined more closely, differences are clearly visible suggesting that the policies and ideology were subject to change.

Prior to the rule of Stalin, Lenin had introduced far reaching social reforms that sought to promote greater levels of equality and rights for women in the newly founded Soviet Union. These included greater working opportunities, and rights to divorce. Stalin continued this commitment when in power. The equality of men and women in the Soviet Union was regularly portrayed in Stalinist propaganda such as the *Worker and Kolkhoz Woman* sculpture made in 1937 showing both genders working together for the strength of the Soviet Union. In a similar vein, Mao's rule over China began with the introduction of the 1950 Marriage Law, which provided legal rights and protection to women in the country. This included the official ending of concubinage, arranged marriages and provided the ability to obtain a divorce. Similar to the Soviet Union, this therefore granted women more social rights than before. This reflects how Stalin and Mao empowered

Annotations:
- Clear opener.
- Indication of the argument to be presented in the essay.
- Relevant example here but more specific details could be provided.
- Relevant example provided.

women in order to further pursue modernization of their respective countries. However, during the mid-1930s we can observe a different trend under Stalin's rule as he brought in the Great Retreat, which sought to reinforce family values and move away from the earlier liberalizing policies of his predecessor.

> *This point could be developed further.*
>
> *Indication of next stage of the essay and a relevant example of a contrast point.*

The answer has regular comparative points, which are clear to follow, showing good structure and historical awareness. Relevant evidence is used to support the analysis. However, some areas of the response need further explanation and justification.

Industrialization in both the Soviet Union and China led to a range of changes for women in society. Mao had remarked that 'women hold up half the sky' indicating that he saw their role as equal to men in the building of a socialist state. Within the Soviet Union, Stalin's mass industrialization and collectivization projects of the 1930s saw a rapidly expanded role of women in the workforce. In China, employment also increased, with the numbers of women in the workforce quadrupling by the end of Mao's rule.

However, attitudes did not necessarily change despite the more progressive policies towards women in both the Soviet Union and China. In fact, one perspective suggests that women's lives may have become more difficult due to high demands of both work and the home. This would suggest that patriarchal gender roles may have continued despite the legal improvements for women. This is reflected in the expression that girl babies were viewed as 'a thousand ounces of gold' compared with boy babies being seen as 'a million ounces of gold' in China; laws may change but attitudes may stay the same.

When Stalin launched the Great Retreat, it can be observed that a more traditional view of gender and the family was becoming policy in the Soviet Union. Abortion was discouraged and later made illegal during the Second World War. Divorce was made more difficult and there were encouragements to increase the birth rate. These changes were not seen in China, the process of collectivization during the Great Leap Forward weakened the family unit due to a restructuring of living arrangements for people. Further, during the height of the Cultural Revolution, the role of the family was again diminished. Young people were encouraged to speak out against their parents and show their love for Mao. Therefore, clear differences are evident in the status of treatment of women between the two authoritarian states.

> *Clear explanatory point.*
>
> *Use of statistic as evidence.*
>
> *This could be more specific.*
>
> *Relevant example with explanation.*
>
> *Clear link back to the question.*

There is a good use of compare and contrast within this response, the student is able to use relevant examples to develop an argument. Some points are developed with detail but not all. There is an awareness of perspectives.

Exam practice

Now it's your turn to try some compare and contrast questions:

1. Compare and contrast the role of foreign policy on the maintenance of power of two authoritarian states from different regions.
2. Compare and contrast the methods used to establish authoritarian states across two authoritarian states.

Cuba under Fidel Castro, 1959–2006

'A revolution is a struggle to the death between the future and the past', remarked **Fidel Castro** in 1959, reflecting on the circumstances surrounding his successful takeover in Cuba that year. The **Cuban Revolution** of 1959 was a turning point in the history of the country which brought the nationalist, **guerrilla** leader, Fidel Castro, and his supporters into power. An iconic leader, known to the world, his rule lasted to the start of the twenty-first century and was defined by many things including a strained relationship with the USA, commitments to looking after impoverished people in society and fierce repression of any opposition.

Castro's rise to power

Revised

■ Conditions leading to the rise to power of Castro

The success of Castro's revolution indicates the importance of the methods used to take power in Cuba, but there were a variety of social, economic and political conditions that made revolution more likely.

■ Economic conditions

- Prior to Castro's rise to power, Cuba's economy was relatively strong in comparison to pre-existing standards in **Latin America**.
- This was largely due to the importance of sugar farming, which was the foundation of the Cuban economy. Cuba's sugar industry had been of significance under Spanish colonization and continued to increase in the twentieth century after independence. It was a major employer on the island.
- The main consumer of Cuban sugar, in the first half of the twentieth century, was the USA. This meant, for better or for worse, that Cuba depended on US imports of their sugar.
- For example, the **Smoot–Hawley Tariff Act** of 1930 negatively impacted Cuba as the Act sought to reduce and set limits on American imports.
- Cuba's economic dependency on the USA was seen by many Cubans as holding the country back and gave voice to opposition movements that developed prior to the Cuban revolution.

■ Impact of war and colonial legacy

- Although of limited importance when examining the rise to power of Castro, a long-term cause of the revolution can be seen in the impact of the **Spanish–American War** of 1898.
- Before independence, Cuba had been under the colonial control of Spain since Columbus had arrived in 1492.
- Subsequently, there had been a range of independence movements and wars throughout Cuba's history, including the **1868–79 Wars of Independence** which ended with Spain promising to bring about more reform.
- The 1898 Spanish–American War led to Spain giving up all claims to Cuba.
- However, the USA replaced the Spanish by stipulating a range of terms for Cuban independence.
- These were the **Platt Amendments** of 1901 and 1903, which included the right of the USA to intervene militarily in Cuba and the lease of **Guantánamo Bay**.
- Cuba allied with the USA during the Second World War, which brought the two countries closer.

Castro's rise to power

ECONOMIC CONDITIONS: SOURCE INVESTIGATION

Examine Sources 1–3 below and then have a go at the questions on this page.

SOURCE 1

A political cartoon from 1901 representing the Platt Amendments of the early twentieth century.

ENCOURAGING THE CHILD.
UNCLE SAM.—That's right, my boy! Go ahead! But, remember, I'll always keep a Father's eye on you!

SOURCE 2

Extract from Vladimir Lenin, *Imperialism, The Highest Stage of Capitalism*, Progress Publishers, Moscow, 1916 (available at www.marxists.org/archive/lenin/works/1916/imp-hsc/pref02.htm).

Capitalism has grown into a world system of colonial oppression and of the financial strangulation of the overwhelming majority of the population of the world by a handful of 'advanced' countries. And this 'booty' is shared between two or three powerful world plunderers armed to the teeth.

SOURCE 3

Extract from a newspaper article by Richard Wong, 'Cuba's Sugar Exports Help Explain the Rise of Fidel Castro', *South China Morning Post*, 2016 (available at www.scmp.com/business/article/2052134/cubas-sugar-exports-help-explain-rise-fidel-castro).

Scholars have offered two interpretations regarding [the economic and political relationships with the USA] and the origins of the Cuban Revolution. Left-wing scholars blame the widespread economic inequality, exploitation, and dependence on the US as the underlying economic cause that invited revolution. Most leading scholars of the revolution counter that Cuba was not suffering from economic recession in the months before the rise of Castro's July 26th Movement and that instead, the crisis was caused by the constitutional illegitimacy of the Batista dictatorship, a popular demand to restore democracy, and a loss of faith in a corrupt and sterile political system.

A major oversight in both interpretations is the neglect of the effects of increased trade protection in the US against Cuban sugar. Eighty per cent or more of Cuba's exports consisted of sugar and more than half was exported to the US. Both sides benefited, with Cuba helping the US to stabilise sugar prices by absorbing variations in the size of the US market in return for all the quota rights from future growth of the US sugar market. However, during the 1950s, US domestic producers began to demand their own share of this growth and in 1956 Congress revised Cuba's quota sharply downwards.

1. What is the message of Source 1? What impact do you think the Platt Amendment to the Cuban constitution would have on Cuba's sense of national identity?

2. In what ways would Lenin's writings as highlighted in Source 2 strike a chord with Cubans?

3. What perspectives are provided in Source 3 to explain the opposition to Batista's regime (see page 80 for information on Batista)?

4. In what ways can economic conditions be viewed as a major contributory factor to the Cuban revolution? What might be some limitations of this perspective?

5 Cuba under Fidel Castro, 1959–2006

■ Weakness of the political system
- The Cuban revolution was an uprising against the government of **Fulgencio Batista**.
- Batista had ruled Cuba as the president from 1940 to 1944, and as head of the armed forces from 1934 to 1940, where he wielded significant political power.
- Batista was voted out of power in 1944 and he spent some time in the USA.
- Batista later ruled from 1952 to 1959; this time he took power by the means of a **military coup**. From here on he ruled as a dictator.
- One of his first moves was to suspend parts of the 1940 constitution of Cuba, which had brought more progressive policies into place.
- Batista's policies favoured the interests of richer people in Cuban society, and in the 1950s he did little to provide for poorer people.
- Corruption increased in Cuba, especially in Havana, the capital. Batista's connections with the Mafia in the USA made matters worse. Gambling, drugs and prostitution all increased during his rule.
- Batista's government was also repressive of civil liberties, using violence against opposition.
- Batista's regime steadily grew in unpopularity. Havana University was a centre of opposition to his rule, with students often holding protests against the corrupt government.
- His regime lost favour with the USA due to the corruption. US President **John F. Kennedy** described his rule as a 'brutal, bloody and despotic dictatorship'.

■ Social division
- The Batista regime exacerbated the social divisions in Cuban society.
- Cuba was a comparatively wealthy country in Latin America but it was the ruling class who took most of the riches.
- Batista's policies in the 1950s favoured these groups, making society more uneven and unjust.
- Furthermore, Cuban society was racially divided, with richer Spanish and white Cubans enjoying most of the privileges, while black Cubans often lived in poverty. This social division had existed for a long time, with the eastern provinces of Cuba, such as **Oriente**, being significantly poorer than the west, where Havana was located.
- Opposition to Batista's regime was connected to social division, and there was increasing interest in socialism and communism. Farm workers who worked the land were also a source of opposition, especially given the huge profits that were made by the **plantation** owners.

SOURCE 4

A photograph of a slum area of Havana in 1954. A casino is located in the background.

MIND MAP

Create a mind map on the conditions affecting Cuba prior to Castro's revolution. You should have sections on the following:

- economic conditions
- weakness of the political system
- social division
- the impact of war.

You can use the following template to help you with the design for this task.

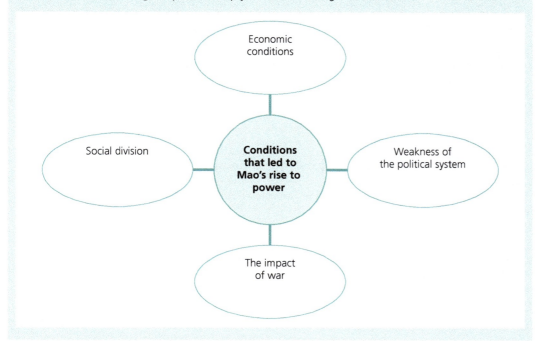

COMPLETE THE PARAGRAPH

Look at the following paragraph starters, then have a go at completing the paragraphs to practise writing about the importance of existing conditions for the rise to power of Castro.

> The political conditions and environment in Cuba during the 1950s made revolution more likely; this was largely due to the rule of Fulgencio Batista …
>
>
>
> In many ways Cuba was a divided society; there were…

Writing help: when writing a paragraph, it is a good idea to make a link back to the original essay question. This allows you to show both analysis and evaluation. Making links gives your answer a good focus and allows you to develop a clear line of argument.

5 Cuba under Fidel Castro, 1959–2006

Methods leading to the rise to power of Castro

The conditions in Cuba under Batista's rule gave rise to opposition groups, most importantly the challenge by Fidel Castro and his followers. Throughout the 1950s, Castro worked in different ways to overthrow the Batista regime, eventually succeeding in 1959.

Castro's early life

- Born on 13 August 1926 in Oriente Province, Castro was the son of a landowner born into a relatively wealthy Cuban family. He was a keen baseball player in his youth.
- Castro had studied law at Havana University during the 1940s, and later became a lawyer.
- Prior to his revolutionary activities in Cuba, he had been involved in failed uprisings in both the Dominican Republic and Colombia. In the Dominican Republic he participated in an attempted ousting of the dictator **Rafael Trujilo**.
- Castro was active politically early on; he had joined the socialist Cuban political party, **Partido Ortodox**, in 1947. By the early 1950s, Castro's influence had increased through his activism and he planned to run as a candidate for Cuba's House of Representatives.
- After Batista's military coup of 1952, this option was no longer open to him and he began looking into ways to take power by force.

The use of force: Moncada Barracks attack

- Force played a major role in the Cuban Revolution, beginning with the **Moncada Barracks attack** on the 26 July 1953.
- This was an attack by Castro and his followers on the barracks near the town of Santiago, which was the residence of large numbers of Batista's military forces.
- The idea behind the attack was to strike the new regime early on before it had the chance to establish its power.
- However, the attack failed. Castro and his followers were significantly outnumbered. In addition, they simply did not have the military training to succeed in this type of mission.
- Fidel Castro and his brother **Raúl Castro** were arrested and many of their followers were killed.

The role of leaders

Castro's trial

- Castro was put on trial after the failed attacks on Moncada Barracks. The trial was in many ways a public relations success for Castro. He made the famous **History will absolve me** speech (see Source 5 opposite), which helped to spread his ideological message and was later turned into a book.
- Castro's speech included a series of aims for Cuba, including land redistribution, bringing back the Cuban constitution and making education more widely accessible. This increased his popularity with many Cubans.
- Castro was given a prison term of fifteen years but was released in 1955, less than two years after his initial conviction. Batista granted **amnesty** to all of the prisoners at this point and they were freed.

The role of Ernesto 'Che' Guevara

After being freed from prison, Castro travelled to Mexico with his followers to regroup and formulate the next stage of his plans to overthrow Batista's regime. At this point, Castro's group was known as the **26 July Movement** (or **M-26-7**) in honour of the Moncada episode. While in Mexico, Castro met the revolutionary **Ernesto 'Che' Guevara**.

- Guevara was a committed anti-capitalist and revolutionary who had trained as a doctor.
- He had moved away from a conventional career as a doctor after his experiences travelling in South America.
- While in Guatemala, Guevara had witnessed the overthrow of the democratically elected President **Jacobo Árbenz** in a military coup backed by the **CIA** in 1954. This increased Guevara's hatred of the USA.
- Guevara met Castro in Mexico and they began working together on how to overthrow Batista's government. Guevara was particularly important for placing an emphasis on the use of guerrilla warfare tactics and working to gain popular support from the people of Cuba.
- Guevara sailed back to Cuba with Castro on the *Granma* yacht in November 1956. The plan was for a successful landing in Cuba where they would quickly take the city of Santiago and inspire an uprising all over Cuba.

- The *Granma* expedition failed, however. The conditions during the crossing from Mexico were very challenging, the boat was overloaded with people and Batista's forces were waiting for them when they arrived on the Cuban mainland.
- Only twelve members of the 26 July Movement evaded capture and fled to the Sierra Maestra mountains.

The role of Raúl Castro

- Fidel Castro's brother Raúl was one of the leaders who had also evaded capture after the *Granma* mission.
- Raúl helped the 26 July Movement by encouraging pre-existing Cuban communist groups to support it. Raúl had built previous connections with the USSR and was a member of the Cuban Communist Party (of the time) in his youth.

SOURCE INVESTIGATION

SOURCE 5

Extract from Fidel Castro's 'History will absolve me' speech made during his trial in 1953 (available at www.marxists.org/history/cuba/archive/castro/1953/10/16.htm).

There are two hundred thousand peasant families who do not have a single acre of land to cultivate to provide food for their starving children ….

A revolutionary government with the backing of the people and the respect of the nation, after cleaning the various institutions of all venal and corrupt officials, would proceed immediately to industrialize the country, mobilizing all inactive capital, currently estimated at about 500 million dollars, through the National Bank and the Agricultural, Industrial and Development Bank, and submitting this mammoth task to experts and men of absolute competence, completely removed from all political machinations, for study, direction, planning and realization … A revolutionary government would solve the housing problem by cutting all rents in half; by providing tax exemptions on homes inhabited by the owners; by tripling taxes on rented homes; by tearing down hovels and replacing them with modern multiple dwelling buildings; and by financing housing all over the island on a scale heretofore unheard of; with the criterion that, just as each rural family should possess its own tract of land, each city family should own its own home or apartment … Finally, a revolutionary government would undertake the integral reform of the educational system, bringing it in line with the foregoing projects with the idea of educating those generations who will have the privilege of living in a happy land.

5 According to Source 5, what were some of the aims that Fidel Castro had for Cuba if his movement was to take power?
___
___

6 In what ways do you think these aims would be popular with people? Try to make comparison points with Batista's rule.
___
___

THE ROLE OF LEADERS

- Create a short profile of the three leaders of the 26 July Movement to reflect on their roles in the Cuban Revolution.
- Use information from this section to help you to develop your ideas here.

Fidel Castro

Role in the Cuban Revolution?

Ernesto 'Che' Guevara

Role in the Cuban Revolution?

Raúl Castro

Role in the Cuban Revolution?

5 Cuba under Fidel Castro, 1959–2006

■ Persuasion, coercion and propaganda
- From November 1956 to the end of 1958, the remaining members of the 26 July Movement were based in the Sierra Maestra mountains in Oriente province, on the eastern side of Cuba.
- They were able to gradually build support from the people living in these areas, in accordance with Guevara's principles of working with and looking after poorer people in society. They worked to gain the support of the *guajiros*, Cuban agricultural workers, by providing medical skills to those in need and helping people with their work.
- Propaganda was also used effectively to increase the popular appeal of the movement. Interviews with Castro painted him and his movement in a positive light in comparison to the corrupt and brutal Batista. In 1957, CBS News in the USA did a special feature called 'The Story of Cuba's Jungle Fighters', which increased the iconic status of the revolutionaries.
- Castro and Guevara had revolutionary appeal around the world due to their public image.
- Guevara set up a newspaper, *El Cubano Libre*, to spread their ideas. Radio broadcasts were also an effective tool for the movement.

■ Ideology
- Primarily, Castro's ideology was nationalistic. He wanted a more independent Cuba that was not reliant on other nations, especially the USA. This had long-term roots connecting with the economic interdependence of the two nations as well as the independence movements that had existed in Cuba under Spanish colonial control. Castro was influenced by Cuban nationalist and intellectual **José Martí**.
- Castro also had a strong commitment to social justice, seeing the plight of poorer members of society as the priority for reforming Cuba. Policies such as land redistribution, provision of education and health care reflect this priority.
- However, it must be noted that Castro did not align himself strongly with Marxism–Leninism until he was actually in power. He had joined the socialist Orthodox Party, which indicates that socialism may be a better description of his ideological position before taking power; however, this can also be debated.

■ The use of force: the overthrow of Batista's regime
As mentioned on page 80, Batista's regime became increasingly unpopular due to the increasing corruption and repression of the people. The USA eventually turned away from Batista for these reasons. Generally, there was increasing sympathy and popular support for the 26 July Movement from wider sections of Cuban society:

- Force continued to play an important role, with skirmishes and battles between Castro and Batista.
- The use of guerrilla tactics was important to the continued success of the movement, as it was able to use the terrain effectively and appeal to the local populations. The movement was able to win important battles in 1958, including the **Battle of La Plata** in July 1958.
- By the end of 1958, the different revolutionary leaders effectively controlled different areas of Cuba, with Raúl Castro in control of the **Sierra Cristal** in the south-east, Guevara in control of central **Escambray** and Fidel Castro in control of Oriente in the east.
- Eventually, Batista's power slipped away from him; the loss of support from the USA was a decisive factor, as was the increased popular discontent with his rule. Other opposition groups to Batista came to support the 26 July Movement, including many student groups and political groups.
- In January 1959, Castro arrived in Havana victorious, with a popular reception. Batista had fled to the Dominican Republic.

SOURCE INVESTIGATION

SOURCE 6

This enduring propaganda image of Guevara is displayed on Cuba's Ministry of the Interior building in Havana.

7 How does Source 6 help us to understand the importance of the revolutionary image of the leaders of the Cuban revolution?
___
___

8 How would Source 7 serve as propaganda to a) promote the 26 July Movement and b) increase the unpopularity of Batista's rule?
___
___
___

SOURCE 7

Extract from Ernesto Guevara, 'Rebel Triumph is Clearly in Sight', an article in *El Cubano Libre*, January 1958 (available from www.themilitant.com/1996/603/603_25.html).

Up until then we saw in each peasant a potential informer; we saw in each peasant hut a threat to our security. We ate boiled malanga or yucca, often without salt or lard. We had still not understood the enormous capacity of struggle of the Cuban peasant. In response to the threats, the mistreatment, the burning of homes, and murder, they responded by supporting us with greater enthusiasm, giving us their children as combatants and guides, and letting us use their houses, all as a contribution to the cause.

Afterward came the battle of Uvero, where we achieved a great though painful triumph, costing us the lives of seven of our comrades.

The subsequent forced evacuation of peasants by the government was the pretext for a thousand crimes, robberies, and abuses against them. Again the peasants responded with renewed support to the cause of the July 26 Movement.

Our fair treatment toward the peasantry – respecting their property, paying for what we consumed, tending their sick, helping those most in need – was the total opposite of the government's bestial policy.

MIND MAP

On page 81 you created a mind map on the conditions that made Cuba more likely to experience revolution. Now create a second mind map on the methods used by Castro and his followers. You should have sections on the following:

- role of leaders
- force
- propaganda
- ideology
- persuasion and coercion.

ESSAY QUESTIONS

Read the following essay questions and have a go at writing a plan or answer the question to help you to prepare for your Paper 2 examination:

1 Examine the role of leaders in the establishment of two authoritarian states.
2 In what ways do weak political systems and economic problems favour the rise of authoritarian states?
3 Compare and contrast the methods used by two leaders in the establishment of authoritarian states.

Castro's consolidation and maintenance of power

Fidel Castro was appointed as the prime minister of Cuba on 16 February 1959; the revolution had succeeded. Castro now faced the task of securing his control over Cuba and implementing policies to maintain the new government. This involved a range of challenges, including the relationship with the USA. This section will examine a range of methods used by Castro to consolidate and maintain his power.

Charismatic leadership and the use of propaganda

- Central to the success of the Cuban Revolution and its consolidation over the country was the role of Fidel Castro as leader, as well as other prominent leaders like Che Guevara.
- There was strict control of the media, with censorship. The official newspaper was named *Granma* after the yacht that had taken the revolutionaries from Mexico to Cuba.
- The *Granma* newspaper was used to generally promote the successes of Castro's rule.
- Radio was also used to promote Marxism and independence movements in other parts of the world. **Radio Havana** was set up in 1961, very shortly after Castro took power.
- Billboards and posters were used all over Cuba to promote speeches and ideological messages to the people.
- Many street and graffiti artists in Cuba reinforced the cult of personality of Fidel Castro by drawing revolutionary images of him in cities such as Havana and Santiago.
- Castro and Guevara's images were popular across the world (and still are) with people who identified with the revolution, further supporting the authority of their rule.

Legal methods

- Once in power, Castro sought to create the new government systems for the running of Cuba. These included the setting up of the **Council of Ministers**, which worked as the highest branch of government, with Castro working as the prime minister.
- Castro did not restore the 1940 constitution as he initially thought he would. Castro governed without a written constitution until 1976 (see page 94).
- Trade union leaders were replaced with people who were known to be pro-Castro.
- The 26 July Movement incorporated the Cuban Communist Party into its membership and many of the party members became government officials. This move weakened ties with the USA, which increasingly saw Castro as a communist leader.

Foreign policy under Castro

Relations with the USA

Castro's relationship with the USA defined Cuban and world history in the early years of his power. Although the USA had tentatively supported Castro over Batista in the final years of the Cuban Revolution, the relationship quickly soured thereafter:

- Castro's anti-Americanism was quickly evident in the seizing of assets and expulsion of companies that were based in Cuba. These included Texaco, Coca-Cola and Standard Oil.
- The USA removed its diplomatic recognition of the new Cuban administration as a result of this and many American policy makers were concerned about the nature of regime, seeing a communist state in their backyard.
- Castro had made agreements with the Soviet leader Nikita Khrushchev, which brought the two closer both diplomatically and economically. This contributed to American fears over the rise of communist governments in the Americas.

Castro's consolidation and maintenance of power

CHALLENGES FACING CASTRO

- As you work through this section, consider the major challenges facing Castro.
- Think about Castro's approach to these different challenges. In what ways did they strengthen or weaken his rule over Cuba?

Challenge	Why would this contribute to his consolidation and maintenance of power?	How did Castro fare? Did his policies strengthen or weaken his position in Cuba?
Setting up political systems		
Controlling media, censorship		
Relationship with the USA		
Relationship with the USSR		
The economy		
Promoting revolution and independence movements in the developing world		
Dealing with opposition		
Surveillance and control of the Cuban people		
Implementing social policies for example literacy campaigns		

WRITING AN INTRODUCTION

Examine the successes and failures of one authoritarian state in the consolidation and maintenance of its rule.

Consider the introduction on this page, thinking about its relative strengths and weaknesses as an introduction to a Paper 2 essay. In addition, pay attention to the annotations which highlight some positives. Once you have done this, consider writing your own introduction to the question to practise this skill.

> By January 1959, Fulgencio Batista had fled Cuba and the 26 July Movement had arrived in Havana to announce the beginning of its rule. Under the leadership of Fidel Castro, the revolutionaries had successfully taken control of Cuba. Once in power, they faced the new challenge of consolidating and maintaining their control over the country. Known to the world, Fidel Castro maintained power until the early twenty-first century (he retired in 2008), so it is clear that he was successful in this process. However, there were many challenges that faced Castro that at different times weakened his position. These included Cuba's relationship with the USA and the performance of the economy.

- The student provides a hook into the essay by starting in 1959.
- Clearly identifies the focus of the essay on the consolidation and maintenance of power.
- Shows the direction that this essay will take in terms of the challenges facing Cuba. However, the introduction does not mention the successes.

5 Cuba under Fidel Castro, 1959–2006

The Bay of Pigs invasion, 1961

- After Castro took power, many Cubans fled from the island, including many wealthy Cubans who had benefited from the Batista regime.
- Many of these people travelled to Guatemala to begin training for a counterinsurgency to take Cuba back from Castro.
- These **Cuban émigrés** received training from the CIA and they organized the attack to land at the **Bay of Pigs** in Cuba.
- Authorized by the new US president, John F. Kennedy, the Bay of Pigs invasion in April 1961 was a total failure.
- It resulted in embarrassment for the USA and later led to Castro publicly announcing Cuba as a communist state following Marxism–Leninism. Castro stated on 2 December 1961: 'I am a Marxist–Leninist and shall be one until the end of my life.'
- This declaration brought Cuba and the USSR closer together, with Khrushchev increasing aid and military supplies to Castro.

The Cuban Missile Crisis

One of the key moments in the Cold War, the **Cuban Missile Crisis**, provides an insight into Castro's position between the two superpowers. For a time, Cuba was at the very centre of the world's attention:

- In October 1962, American spy planes brought back footage of mid-range nuclear missiles installed in Cuba. They had been installed by the USSR.
- This brought fear and panic to Washington. The American government saw this as a direct threat to the USA. Kennedy decided to install a **naval blockade** on Cuba as a response that sought to show resolve without bringing about the use of the weapons.
- Khrushchev complained of double standards, given the location of American nuclear missiles based in Turkey.
- After negotiations, on 28 October, Khrushchev agreed to remove the missiles from Cuba.
- Guevara and Castro, in many ways, were bystanders in this dispute, but Castro claimed a 'moral victory'. The missile crisis did little to improve the relations between the USA and Cuba, with the continuation of the embargo over Cuba.
- Overall, the worsening of relations with the USA had a mixed effect on Castro's power. He took victory from the failings of the Bay of Pigs but found his country increasingly isolated as a result of the embargo, leading to increased reliance on the USSR.
- Poor relations with the USA would define Castro's leadership for the majority of his rule.

Castro's foreign policy during the 1970s

Castro's foreign policy was not entirely dominated by its poor relations with the USA. We can also see a range of foreign policy moves by Castro that reflect on his aims for promoting independence and revolutionary movements around the world. Castro was especially keen on supporting Marxist groups in developing countries. The following timeline shows some examples of Cuba's role in other parts of the world.

Years	Castro's actions
1971	Castro supported the government of **Salvador Allende**, the recently elected president in Chile. He visited the country and sought to build diplomatic relations. Allende was overthrown by a military coup in 1973, which brought an end to this relationship
1975	Castro, in line with wanting to support the development of Marxism in developing countries, pledged support to the Marxists fighting a civil war in Angola. He committed Cuban troops to this effort
1975–7	During the mid-1970s, Castro conducted a wide variety of visits to countries in Africa to support different Marxist and independence movements. This was connected to his anti-imperialist worldview. Commitments included sending troops, doctors and teachers in different capacities. Countries that Castro visited included Somalia, Tanzania and Libya
1979	Castro supported the **Sandinistas** in Nicaragua after they had seized power in a revolution. This brought Castro into indirect conflict with the USA, which supported the CIA-backed **Contras** to overthrow the Sandinistas
1979	A successful moment for Castro was his appointment as secretary-general of the **Non-Aligned Movement** in 1979

Overall, the 1970s saw Cuba having a heavy involvement in a range of independence movements in developing countries which fitted with Castro's principles. During the 1980s, Castro's foreign policy moves were dampened by the actions of US President Ronald Reagan as well as the more conciliatory policies of Mikhail Gorbachev. The end of the Cold War led to the increased diplomatic isolation of Cuba, and the Special Period (as discussed on page 94) which saw more limited foreign policy moves.

SOURCE INVESTIGATION

Look at the sources below and answer the questions which follow.

SOURCE 8

Announcement of the US embargo on Cuba in 1962 by President John F. Kennedy (available at www.presidency.ucsb.edu/ws/?pid=58824).

Hereby prohibit, effective 12:01 A.M., Eastern Standard Time, February 7, 1962, the importation into the United States of all goods of Cuban origin and all goods imported from or through Cuba; and I hereby authorize and direct the Secretary of the Treasury to carry out such prohibition, to make such exceptions thereto, by license or otherwise, as he determines to be consistent with the effective operation of the embargo hereby proclaimed, and to promulgate such rules and regulations as may be necessary to perform such functions.

SOURCE 9

Castro's response to the Bay of Pigs invasion, 1961, where he outlined different examples of US aggression towards Cuba (available at www.marxists.org/history/cuba/archive/castro/1961/04/23.htm).

Then they turned to backing terrorists and saboteurs. A campaign to destroy our stores and factories began. Now that the people own the installations, sabotage comes. When the wealthy owned them, there was no sabotage. But now that people own the establishments, the CIA goes into action. There is a sabotage campaign.

They organize sabotage against our wealth, they burn [sugar] cane. They began to send planes over to burn it, but there was so much scandal that they changed tactics. They began to stir up counterrevolutionary groups, using formed soldiers, the worst elements. The worst were those who directed the second Escambray front. They sent them all kinds of arms. You have seen the display of weapons in the Civil Plaza. These worms, in a few weeks, got a thousand weapons, while we, in our battles, had to acquire arms one by one. They sent arms by air, by sea. And we are [unreadable text] seizing these arms.

Aggression began economically, with maneuvers in sugar and an economic blockade; then came sabotage and counterrevolutionary guerrillas.

The United States has no right to meddle in our domestic affairs. We do not speak English and we do not chew gum. We have a different tradition, a different culture, our own way of thinking. Our national characteristics are different. We have no borders with anybody. Our frontiers are the sea, very clearly defined.

Only because it is a big country did the United States take the right to commit that series of brutalities against Cuba. How can the crooked politicians and the exploiters have more rights than the people? What right does a rich country have to impose its yoke on our people? Only because they have might and no scruples; they do not respect international rules. They should have been ashamed to be engaged in this battle of Goliath against David – and to lose it besides.

SOURCE 10

Nikita Khrushchev (third from left) and Fidel Castro (far right) in Moscow in 1964. The Cuban–Soviet trade deal was signed in 1964.

9 What impact would the embargo on Cuba, as shown in Source 8, have on Cuba's economy?

10 What examples does Castro outline in his speech in Source 9 of how the USA has shown aggression towards Cuba?

11 How might the David and Goliath analogy, used in Source 9, help to promote support for Castro internationally?

12 What can you learn from Source 10 about the Soviet–Cuban relationship?

Economic policies

On the whole, the first decade of Castro's rule was full of problems associated with economic development and production. Although he inherited a range of problems, he was also unable to modernize the Cuban economy:

- The sugar industry continued to play a dominant role under Castro. Previously, Cuba had been the leading global provider of sugar, but Castro inherited the industry at a weak stage in its history.
- The lack of modernization, using new technology and farming techniques, as well as the severing of economic ties with the USA, made matters worse.
- Castro also had a lack of skilled workers and managers given the large numbers of Cubans who had emigrated after the revolution. This is sometimes referred to as a **brain drain**.
- Castro made some significant changes to the economy, most notably land reform. He created the **Institute of Agrarian Reform** which carried out the process of land redistribution, breaking up the *latifundias*.
- Castro also developed a range of policies to make conditions for lower-paid workers easier, including the creation of government subsidies to reduce rents and the building of public housing.
- Castro also nationalized the sugar industry.

Economic problems

Diversification	The Ten-Million Ton Harvest
A failure of the early years was Castro's attempts to diversify the Cuban economy. Trying to break down the reliance on sugar by developing a wider range of industries was a good idea in theory but ultimately failed. To make matters worse, the efforts to try out new crops caused problems for the land when the focus returned to sugar, subsequently disrupting the sugar harvests	The decision to focus on sugar due to the failings of **diversification** led to a later call for a **Ten-Million Ton Harvest**. In this powerful propaganda message, Castro encouraged a collective and nationalist effort to maximize production. This was encouraged by the creation of state farms which were increased in size after the nationalization of the sugar industry. However, the harvest intended for 1970 failed to hit its target for a variety of reasons, including a lack of skilled farm workers and corruption

Castro's consolidation and maintenance of power

MATCH THE TERMS TO THE DESCRIPTIONS

Term	Definition
Institute of Agrarian Reform	Policy which sought to reduce Cuba's reliance on sugar by developing other domestic industries
Latifundias	National target, proclaimed by Fidel Castro, to be achieved in 1970
Diversification	An organization set up to oversee the land reform policies after the Agrarian Reform Law of 1959
Ten-Million Ton Harvest	Large areas of land, usually taking the form of a plantation. These were limited under Castro's agrarian reforms

WRITING PRACTICE

- Let's return to the essay that was considered in the activity on page 87.
- This time, practise writing a paragraph about the economic policies of Castro in relation to his consolidation of power.

Examine the successes and failures of one authoritarian state in the consolidation and maintenance of its rule.

Below are some factors that you might want to consider in your paragraph.

Positives for consolidation	Negatives for consolidation
• Positive trading relationship with the USSR	• Poor economic relationship with the USA
• Establishment of land reform	• Lack of diversification and dominance of sugar industry
• Policies to help poorer people, for example rent reductions, reductions in unemployment	• Failure to meet economic targets

You could use the following prompts to help you to structure your paragraph:

A difficult area for Castro after taking power was ensuring that Cuba was able to make economic progress under the new government. A major factor that affected the Cuban economy was connected to its worsening relationship with the USA.

However, a range of measures were introduced that allowed Castro to establish systems of economic reform and planning. The land reform policies, for instance.

Overall though, it seems that the economic performance of the country brought about more uncertainty, as evidenced in ....

Opposition to Castro's rule

When Castro arrived in Havana in January 1959, he was cheered in the streets and there was popular support for the new government. However, his rule was often highly repressive towards those seen as opposition:

- One of Castro's first acts was the public trials and executions of Batista's supporters, often carried out by firing squads. Many people were killed without trial.
- Castro's repression extended to people he described as anti-socials, an intolerant approach to dealing with people whose needs did not align with his revolutionary fervour. This image disconnects with the imagery of Fidel and Che as 'revolutionary heroes' in the West.

Opposition to Castro grew and the following were some of the people disaffected with the regime:

- Those who lost out economically under his rule, including landowners, factory owners and industrialists.
- Agricultural labourers who were opposed to the creation of the state farms.
- Writers, artists and intellectuals who did not like the imposition of censorship.
- Leaders of trade unions who wanted more representation for different worker groups.
- Those who were pro-American in Cuba or had connections with the US Cuban émigrés.
- Overseas opposition, as seen in the Bay of Pigs invasion.

Treatment of opposition

- Castro dealt with repression forcibly. Opposition groups did not successfully challenge his power base and there was a lack of cohesion between opposition groups.
- Castro was able to build his popularity through policies that brought improvements to people's lives. Propaganda was also used to maintain a positive image of Castro and the state.
- Many Cubans who were in opposition to Castro simply left, often migrating to the USA. Castro introduced some regulations to keep control of the number of people leaving.
- Surveillance organizations were set up to keep people in line. The **Committee for the Defence of the Revolution (CDR)** was set up in 1960 to ensure that different neighbourhoods were adhering to the revolutionary ideas, keeping an eye on anyone who might be in opposition.
- Examples of the treatment of opposition can be seen in the treatment of **Huber Matos** and **Armando Valladares**.
- Huber Matos was a member of the 26 July Movement who was critical of the moves towards communism once the group took power. Matos was accused of treason and spent twenty years in prison, where he suffered tremendous hardships including solitary confinement and torture.
- Armando Valladares was arrested and imprisoned for refusing to put a 'I'm with Fidel' sign on his desk. Like Matos, he suffered terrible hardships in prison. Valladares wrote poetry that gained international attention for revealing the dark side of Castro's Cuba.

Opposition case studies

Mariel Boatlift	Ladies in White
The **Mariel Boatlift** highlights the large number of Cubans who were disaffected with life under Castro. Up until 1980, thousands of Cubans fled the country, often ending up as refugees in the USA. Castro and US President **Jimmy Carter** had come to an agreement to allow this migration to take place. It is estimated that over 100,000 Cubans left during 1980	An event in 2003 known as the **Black Spring** led to the mass arrests of people in Cuba seen to be in opposition to the government, including political activists, journalists and those looking to bring attention to human rights issues. The **Ladies in White**, many of whom were married to those imprisoned, formed shortly afterwards. Wearing white to symbolize peace, they attended church on Sunday and publicly walked through the streets of Havana

Castro's consolidation and maintenance of power

SOURCE INVESTIGATION

- Consider the sources and then complete the table below.
- Think about the information the source provides and how it helps you to understand the treatment of opposition in Cuba.

SOURCE 11

Extract from Armando Valladares, *Against All Hope: A Memoir of Life in Castro's Gulag*, Encounter Books, New York, 2001, page 30.

On January 12, on a firing range located in a small valley called San Juan, at the end of the island in the province of Oriente, hundreds of soldiers from the defeated army of Batista had been lined up in a trench knee-deep and more than fifty yards [45 metres] long. Their hands were tied behind their backs, and they were machine-gunned there where they stood. Then with bulldozers the trenches were turned into mass graves. There had been no trial of any kind for those men.

SOURCE 12

Extract from an article by Yoani Sanchez, 'CDR: Citizen Representation or Political Control?', 28 September 2012, for the Translating Cuba website. Sanchez is writing as someone who was a member of the Committee for the Defence of the Revolution (CDR) in Cuba (available at http://translatingcuba.com/cdr-citizen-representation-or-political-control-yoani-sanchez/).

In short, I grew up as a child of the CDR, although when I reached adulthood I refused to become a militant among its ranks. I lived all this and I don't regret it, because now I can conscientiously say from the inside that all those beautiful moments are dwarfed by the abuse, the injustices, the accusations and control that these so-called committees have visited on me and millions of other Cubans.

I speak of the many young people who were not able to attend university in the years of the greatest ideological extremism because of a bad reference from the president of their CDR. It was enough during a reference check from a school or workplace for some CDRista to say that an individual was 'not sufficiently combative' for them to not be accepted for a better job or a university slot.

It was precisely these neighborhood organizations who most forcefully organized the repudiation rallies carried out in 1980 against those Cubans who decided to emigrate through the port of Mariel in what came to be known on the other shore as the Mariel Boatlift. And today they are also the principal cauldron of the repressive acts against the Ladies in White and other dissidents.

SOURCE 13

Cubans saying their goodbyes while awaiting transportation to the USA. About 125,000 Cubans fled the island between 15 April and 31 October 1980 when Fidel Castro opened the Port of Mariel and announced that anyone who wished to leave could do so.

Castro's political and economic policies, 1970–90

The Cuban constitution, 1976

Between 1959 and 1976, Castro ruled without any legitimate constitutional rule. He decided to introduce a new constitution in 1975 to add legitimacy to his rule and to restructure some of the political systems. Changes included:

- Castro was head of state, serving as president and head of the Cuban Communist Party.
- The constitution stated that Cuba was a single-party, socialist state (as seen in Article 5).
- Commitments to free education and health care were included.
- A system of government with an elected National Assembly, with its members being drawn from local assemblies. Only members of the Communist Party could work at local or national levels.
- The constitution also led to government ministers having more freedom to develop policies, and trade unions gaining more rights.

Rectification

After 1970, another approach that brought about changes to Cuba was the rectification policies:

- These were made in the light of changes that were seen to be required to allow the state to make progress economically and socially.
- Changes included the more widespread adoption of technology in factories and offices, bringing incentives into the workplace to encourage productivity and setting production targets in different industries.
- This led to some economic progress, with the economy growing steadily from 1971 to 1976.
- However, the economy declined after this point, which led to austerity measures.

Austerity

Austerity measures were introduced in the 1980s due to Cuba's poor economic performance. These were the result of the following:

- A continued trade imbalance, with Cuba importing more goods than exporting.
- An over-reliance on the sugar industry.
- A dependency on the USSR for the sale of Cuban goods.
- High levels of debt.

Austerity involved public calls from Castro and the leadership of the Cuban Communist Party to live more frugal lives, not to worry about material needs and to focus on the national interest. It was further evidence of the challenges facing the Cuban economy, which were mirrored in the economic stagnation occurring in the USSR and Eastern European communist states at the time.

The Special Period

In 1989, a series of revolutions led to the collapse of communism in Eastern Europe. Shortly afterwards, the USSR was dissolved and the Cold War was officially over. This situation created problems for Castro, given Cuba's reliance on the USSR. The time after 1989 became known as the Special Period and was characterized by a range of economic difficulties for the Cuban people:

- There was a massive drop in income levels.
- Previously, Cuba had been provided with the majority of its oil from the USSR, so the Special Period also saw a drop in oil supplies arriving into the country.
- Power cuts and fewer resources meant that older forms of transport were used to save energy, including bicycles.
- Rationing was introduced to deal with the food shortages.

These problems led to Castro making political and economic changes in Cuba to maintain the regime. He remained committed to his ideological position. Changes included encouraging more tourism to the country, allowing some religious freedoms and seeking better relations with China.

The end of Fidel Castro's rule

Fidel Castro officially retired in 2008 and his brother Raúl took his place. His final years in power saw an increase in authoritarian repression of those who sought social change in Cuba. The country was blacklisted by the USA and its economy remained in a weakened state. However, Castro's reputation still continues to provoke debate about the different ways that he changed Cuba, which will be explored in the next section.

Castro's consolidation and maintenance of power

SUMMARY REFLECTIONS

- As we reach the end of this section, this is a good opportunity to reflect on how you could connect your understanding to the consolidation and maintenance of Castro's rule.
- The table below provides suggested case studies for different policy areas that were important to Castro's rule.
- Write a reflection on each area to consider its relative importance.

Methods for consolidation and maintenance of power	Possible case studies	Reflection (consider how it would impact Fidel Castro's rule and power)
Political policies	Setting up the Council of Ministers Commitments to Marxism 1976 Constitution	
Economic policies	Land reform Diversification Rectification Austerity Special Period	
Foreign policies	Relations with the USA Relations with the USSR Involvement in developing countries, for example Angola	
Propaganda and charismatic leadership	Control of media Role of Fidel Castro as leader	
Treatment of opposition	Treatment of dissidents Cuban émigrés CDR Black Spring	

WRITING A CONCLUSION

Examine the successes and failures of one authoritarian state in the consolidation and maintenance of its rule.

- When writing a conclusion, it is important to show your overall understanding of the question.
- Ideally, it should show that you have developed a clear line of argument that has been backed up by evidence.
- Take a look at this conclusion. What do you think are the strengths and limitations of the conclusion?

> Overall, what cannot be disputed is Castro's longevity of rule and that his power base was never seriously threatened, with his commitments to poorer people increasing his popularity. We can see that he built a reputation to the Cuban people and to the world as a committed revolutionary and nationalist. However, there was a cost to this; the large number of people who migrated away from Cuba shows the levels of dissatisfaction with his rule, strongly seen in Cuba's poor economic performance. Furthermore, without the use of force and the establishment of strict authoritarian control it is unlikely that his power would have lasted as long as it did.

Castro's domestic policies: aims and results

Treatment of women in Cuba

Before the revolution

Before the revolution, the conditions in Cuba for women were favourable compared to other countries at the time:

- Women had been granted the vote and had employment opportunities in a wide variety of fields.
- The 1940 constitution of Cuba, which had been disbanded by Batista, provided commitments to gender equality.
- Once in power, Castro continued the commitments to gender equality in Cuba.
- Women had played an important role in the success of the 26 July Movement, helping to promote the movement during the Sierra Maestra campaign.
- A prominent activist was **Celia Sánchez**, who worked with the guerrilla fighters by co-ordinating supplies of weapons and medical resources and aiding them during their time in the mountains.

After the revolution

- After the success of the revolution, Castro followed through on his commitments to make gender equality an important part of the new Cuba.
- The **Cuban Women's Federation (FMC)**, set up in 1960, sought to encourage women into the workplace with a variety of incentives.
- Incentives included setting up day-care centres where children could be left, promoting **literacy campaigns**, which were an important part of the education policy, promoting health and hygiene, and teaching useful skills to women.
- By 1975, the FMC had over 4 million members.
- Legally, the **1975 Family Code** was enacted to provide clear guidelines for the law concerning marriage, divorce and childcare. The code sought more equality within marriage, for example Article 25 states that 'Partners must live together, be loyal, considerate, respectful and mutually helpful to each other.'
- A prominent leader for women during Castro's rule was **Vilma Espín**, who helped to write the 1975 Family Code and was in charge of the FMC.
- Criticisms of the progress of women under Castro focus on the conservative nature of the reform, which placed traditional institutions such as marriage at the forefront. The lack of women in the National Congress for Cuba also suggested limited progress.
- A perspective that suggests that the reality for women in Cuba is not equality refers to the term **machismo**. This is a word used to describe the patriarchal aspects of Cuban culture that cannot be eradicated with legal change.
- Finally, conditions for poorer women in Cuba continued to be difficult.

Treatment of minorities in Cuba

On paper, one would expect that the conditions for minority groups in Cuba would have improved under Castro's rule. His commitments to improving the lives of people alongside socialist principles, however, did not properly materialize once in power. A case in point is the lack of improved social conditions for **black Cubans**.

Black Cubans

Black Cubans are a minority of the population who are descended from enslaved people. Black Cubans are on average the poorest in Cuba. They supported Castro, feeling that he would bring greater equality to Cuban society:

- Castro, in speeches, made reference to the end of discrimination in Cuba and the importance of racial equality.
- A major critic of Castro was **Carlos Moore**, who left Cuba in 1963. He felt that little had been done to improve the conditions faced by black Cubans or to remove racism from Cuban society. Moore's 2009 book, *Pichón: Race and Revolution in Castro's Cuba: A Memoir*, describes the lack of progress for black Cubans under Castro. (**Pichón** is a racist term used towards black Cubans.)

Gay/lesbian people

- The treatment of gay/lesbian people in Cuba is a case in point of the repressive and intolerant nature of Castro's rule, especially during the 1960s.
- Early on, labour camps were set up called **Military Units to Aid Production (UMAPs)**. These facilities involved long working days doing agricultural work in very poor conditions.
- Many gay/lesbian people were arrested and put in these camps.
- The camps closed in the late 1960s, but discrimination continued.
- In 1979, homosexual acts were decriminalized; this was more progressive, but did not necessarily improve people's lives in Cuba.
- Writer **Reinaldo Arenas** describes his life and conflict with the Cuban authorities over his sexuality in his 1992 book *Before Night Falls*. He spent time in prison and was part of the Mariel Boatlift that saw many other gay/lesbian people leave Cuba in 1980.

Religious groups

- Jehovah's Witnesses were targeted by Castro's regime, part of a group described as 'social deviants' who ended up in the UMAPs in the 1960s. Practising this religion was outlawed in 1974.
- Other religious groups, especially the dominant Roman Catholic and Protestant Churches, carried on under Castro's rule, but membership of the Communist Party was not allowed for those who practised religion. Religious leaders who were critical of the government were repressed.
- Religious freedom gradually has become more openly tolerated in Cuba.

Castro's domestic policies: aims and results

SOURCE INVESTIGATION

- Using the sources and the information on the opposite page, put together a summary of the conditions facing women in Cuba.
- You should consider the conditions before the revolution, changes brought about by Castro and the results.
- Use the table provided below.

SOURCE 14

Article 26 of the Cuban Family Code (available at http://ufdc.ufl.edu/AA00021904/00001/11j).

Both partners must care for the family they have created and each must cooperate with the other in the education, upbringing and guidance of the children according to the principles of socialist morality. They must participate, to the extent of their capacity or possibilities, in the running of the home, and cooperate so that it will develop in the best possible way.

SOURCE 15

Extract from Elizabeth Stone's introduction to *Women and the Cuban Revolution: Speeches and Documents by Fidel Castro, Vilma Espín and others*, edited by Elizabeth Stone, Pathfinder Press, New York, 1981, page 29.

The struggle of women for equal rights in Cuba is a process. At every stage, underdevelopment has placed obstacles along the way. But since 1959 there have been big leaps forward in all areas – from the right to an education, a job, paid maternity leaves, child care, and abortion to getting rid of prostitution and ending degrading practices such as beauty contests and sexist advertising.

Such impressive gains could not have been achieved except within the context of a deepgoing revolution which not only challenged the oppression of women, but set out to eradicate capitalism – an economic system whose motive force is maximizing profit for a tiny handful who own the productive resources of society – and replace it with an economic system based on maximizing the well-being for all.

SOURCE 16

Number of women in the Cuban Women's Federation, from Michael Lynch, *Access to History for the IB Diploma: Authoritarian states*, second edition, Hodder Education, London, 2015, page 252.

Year	Number of women	Number of branches
1961	17,000	340
1965	584,797	10,694
1970	1,324,751	27,370
1975	4,800,000	46,146

What were conditions for women like in Cuba before the revolution?	What were Castro's aims for the role of women in society?
What changes were brought in?	What were the successes and failures of these policies?

5 Cuba under Fidel Castro, 1959–2006

■ Castro's social policies

Some of the more successful aspects of Castro's rule can be seen in his social policies concerning education and health.

■ Education

- From the outset, education was a priority for Castro. He wanted to increase literacy and provide free, quality education for all.
- In 1961, the literacy campaign was launched. This was a massive project that sought to achieve (or get as near as possible to) 100% literacy in Cuba.
- People were sent to remote areas to teach reading and writing. There were a range of different workers in the campaign: some paid and some voluntary. The campaign was well organized.
- The campaign was a success and Cuba has had very high literacy levels for many years.
- Further, many of the Cuban teachers were sent abroad to help develop literacy in other locations.
- Education, although raising levels of achievement, was also attached to the ideology of the Cuban Communist Party and the national interest.

■ Health policies

- Health care had always been a major focus of the 26 July Movement, especially evident in Guevara's training as a doctor.
- After the revolution, health services were nationalized with commitments to free, universal health care.
- The 1976 Cuban constitution provided these legal guarantees to health care for the Cuban people.
- In the second half of the twentieth century, the doctor–patient ratio became more favourable, life expectancy had increased and infant mortality had reduced.
- Cuban doctors regularly are sent overseas to help in areas of need. In recent years, many Cuban doctors have travelled to west Africa to help with the Ebola crisis.

REVIEW QUESTIONS

Revise your understanding of this chapter by going through these revision questions. Think about areas where you need to spend a bit more time on your revision.

1. How did economic conditions help Castro to take power in Cuba by 1959?
2. What was the nature of Batista's rule during the 1950s?
3. What factors led to the success of the Cuban revolution? What was the role of a) leaders and b) propaganda?
4. What were the features of the Cuban economy under Fidel Castro? What were different examples of successes and failures?
5. How did Castro improve the lives of Cubans?
6. What methods were used by Castro to maintain his rule over Cuba?
7. In what ways was Castro's rule over Cuba repressive?
8. How would you describe Fidel Castro's ideology?
9. Explain Cuba's relationship with the USA and the USSR under Fidel Castro.
10. What impact did the break-up of the USSR and the end of the Cold War have on Cuba?
11. Why might there be different historical interpretations of Fidel Castro's rule?

REFLECTING ON DOMESTIC POLICIES UNDER CASTRO

Complete the following reflection document, which explores both the aims and results of domestic policies under Castro.

Policies and attitudes towards women and the family	Policies and attitudes towards minorities in Cuba	Education policies
Aims:	Aims:	Aims:
Results:	Results:	Results:
Health policies	Economic policies	Political policies
Aims:	Aims:	Aims:
Results:	Results:	Results:

Now consider an essay plan in response to the following question:

Evaluate the successes and failures of domestic policies under one authoritarian state.

From your table, consider what examples you will use to develop an argument. What factors were more successful? What were the reasons for the failings of particular policies? Could you challenge the terminology of success and failure in the context of some of the policies?

Now have a look at the following sample response to the question that focuses on areas of success:

> A clear area of progress due to the policies passed by the Cuban Communist Party can be seen in the areas of education and health. These areas had distinct aims of trying to provide more universal benefits to all Cubans throughout the country. Literacy campaigns to teach the skills of reading and writing were carried out through national schemes such as the 1961 literacy campaign, significantly increasing the educational provision for people in the country. Likewise, in health care, Castro, especially encouraged by Che Guevara, wanted to improve health care, creating more favourable doctor-to-patient ratios. Further evidence of success here can be seen in Cuba's significant role in sending teachers and medical professionals to areas of need in the world.

The student clearly explains an example of domestic policy success with analytical and comparative language. You would expect the student to go further with other examples of success or failures. The student must remember to provide specific evidence throughout the essay.

The student makes a clear point to indicate what will be discussed.

Good, logical and relevant connective between education and health care.

Analytical writing to further highlight the successful nature.

Exam focus

Sample question and answer

- Read the sample response to this essay question and pay attention to the annotations provided.
- Consider the feedback you would give to the essay.
- When you have finished reading the essay, have a look at the essay questions provided and attempt to write a response.

Compare and contrast the methods used by two authoritarian leaders to maintain their rule.

The twentieth century saw many countries adopting communism as their official ideology, starting with Russia in 1917. Two notable communist states were China under Mao Zedong and Cuba under Fidel Castro. These authoritarian states, on opposite sides of the world to each other, needed to use a range of methods to ensure their stability and power base. As shall be seen, both states used similar methods to maintain power, and both experienced challenges associated with foreign policy and economic policies. Overall though, the different contexts of their rule meant that fundamentally these were very distinct authoritarian states from each other.

Mao and Castro both used propaganda and charismatic leadership as methods to maintain their authority over their respective states. The speeches of both leaders were an important unifying point on which people could focus. The words of Castro were used to rally support for the revolution and his plans for Cuba as early on as his trial in 1953 following the failed attack on the Moncada Barracks. Castro spoke out on many things, including the need for universal education and health care, through to his open criticisms of the USA. This was also seen in China; Mao's words were always referenced but at its height, during the Cultural Revolution of the 1960s, this turned to fervour with a cult of personality exceeding anything that was seen in Cuba. The control of the media was an example of a similar methodology; through the use of newspapers, posters and radio, important messages were transmitted to ensure conformity to their rule. Castro's regime, for instance, made use of a newspaper, the 'Granma', which provided stories about the achievements of his rule. Mao's use of socialist realism in posters promoted the role of the people in achieving the aims for China.

Mao and Castro also faced similar challenges while in control, which affected their maintenance of power. The challenge of developing the economies of Cuba and China was a struggle for both leaders. When the Great Leap Forward went wrong, leading to the three bitter years between 1959 and 1961 which included mass starvation of people in the countryside, Mao took a step back from political prominence, allowing more moderate leaders such as Deng Xiaoping and Liu Shaoqi to take more control. Cuba's economic performance faltered for many years during Castro's regime, which encouraged opposition to his rule. Examples of difficulties included the failure to meet the Ten-Million Ton Harvest target in 1970 and the need for austerity measures in the 1980s. However, both leaders maintained their grip on power despite the economic challenges, suggesting that there must have been other more successful policies that helped them to maintain their control.

A major difference between the approaches of Mao and Castro can be seen in their foreign policies. Although both states had a poor relationship with the USA and at times both relied on the USSR, they had different ideas about the role of foreign policy. Within the Chinese context, we see Mao as more concerned with the territorial integrity of China through his many involvements that were close to the borders of China, including the Korean War, Taiwan Straits Crisis and border conflicts with both the USSR and India. Cuba, less concerned about its borders, also played a role in its own region, as seen by Castro's support of the Sandinistas in Nicaragua, but he also took the cause of independence movements and Marxism far away from the shores of Cuba. Castro's involvement in Africa saw him build his reputation as a revolutionary who was interested in the needs of other countries. Mao, however, was more concerned with the domestic situation, and indeed during the Cultural Revolution, China isolated itself from the world.

> Good links to Castro's work in Africa but maybe provide an example.

Force was a feature of both authoritarian states. The laogai in China were set up across the country to hold prisoners who were seen to be in opposition to the CCP. These camps had harsh conditions. Labour camps were also used in Cuba with the creation of the UMAP, which were used to imprison people labelled as 'social deviants', including gay/lesbian people and Jehovah's Witnesses. Both leaders at times increased the repression of people within society to maintain their power, as seen in the Hundred Flowers Campaign in China and the Black Spring in Cuba in 2003. The Hundred Flowers saw Mao openly invite criticism and then repress dissident voices in a crackdown called the Anti-Rightist Campaign. In 2003 in Cuba, the Black Spring saw a wave of arrests of activists who were seen to be in opposition to the Communist Party. However, with Castro's Cuba we see far more examples of conciliatory policies to maintain power. Throughout Castro's rule, many people opposing him were allowed to leave, as seen by the Mariel Boatlift where thousands of Cubans left for the USA in 1980. Further, the easing of restrictions at different times, for example during the Special Period after 1989, is when Castro brought in some further freedoms to the people who were experiencing economic hardship.

> Use of relevant terminology.

> Maybe explain what this stands for.

> Comparison point provided.

> Contrast point.

Overall, both Mao and Castro came to power as very popular leaders and stayed in power without major challenges to their rule. The importance of their charismatic leadership goes a long way in explaining this, especially as they had both been significant figures in their countries' history prior to taking power. Furthermore, we see similar methods for keeping control, including the importance of force, propaganda and social policies. However, the contexts of their rule were very different, both ideologically and also with the nature of their rule. Mao's use of a cult of personality during the Cultural Revolution towards the end of his rule was far more extensive than Castro's who, over time, used a combination of conciliatory and nationalistic messages to maintain his control over Cuba.

> The conclusion argues to a reasoned conclusion but doesn't link back to economic and foreign policy. Generally well argued to this point.

> An analytical, well-structured essay that provides a wide range of examples to support the comparison. There are a range of relevant comparison and contrast points; historical awareness is evident. Some examples could have been further detailed and could have linked to perspectives on Castro's and Mao's historical reputations.

Exam practice

Now it's your turn to try to answer these essay questions:

1. Examine the impact of two authoritarian states on minority groups.
2. Compare and contrast the status and treatment of women in two authoritarian states.
3. To what extent were successful political and economic policies essential to the maintenance of power of authoritarian states?
4. Examine the methods used to consolidate power in two authoritarian states.

Argentina under Juan Perón, 1946–74

Populist leader **Juan Perón** served as the president of Argentina for three terms during the twentieth century. Elected into power in 1946, he served as president of the country for two terms until he was ousted from power in 1955. In 1973, Perón was re-elected president but this was short lived due to his death in 1974. Perón remains a historically divisive leader whose rule brought many benefits to impoverished people in Argentine society, but was also defined by strict measures of authoritarian rule.

Perón's rise to power

Revised

Conditions leading to the rise to power of Perón

Following the war of independence against Spain, the newly independent Argentina developed during the nineteenth century into a relatively prosperous country. However, there were numerous economic, social and political conditions that helped to make Perón's rise to power more likely. This section will explore these conditions.

Long-term social and economic conditions

- By the end of the nineteenth century, the economy of Argentina was performing relatively well. There had been slow growth in the years following independence, but the gradual development of industry and infrastructure had improved the economic situation.
- Of particular note was the importance of the meat export industry for Argentina.
- Socially, there had been a large amount of immigration into Argentina during the nineteenth century from a wide variety of European countries, including Spain, Switzerland and Italy, in large part due to the favourable economic conditions.
- Argentina had a long tradition of rural elites holding great influence in the country; these groups owned large estates, especially in the **Pampas** region, and were known as *estancieros*.
- Subsequently, there was a great deal of inequality in Argentina when considering the vast wealth of the *estancieros*. However, the development of the economy in the nineteenth century had led to the growth of the middle classes in the country, with the city of Buenos Aires reflecting many of the demographic changes.

ESSAY PLANNING

In this section we will work on an essay that is aimed at answering a question on the role that pre-existing conditions had on the rise to power of Juan Perón. Here is the question:

Evaluate the significance of political and economic conditions for the emergence of an authoritarian state in the twentieth century.

Your first task is to make a plan of what you will need to do to answer this question. Go through the following list to help you to formulate your approach to the question.

- Step 1: understanding the command term:
  - The command term for this essay question is *evaluate*. You can refer to the definition on page 6.
  - What approach do you think you will need to focus on for this type of question?
- Step 2: initial ideas for the essay:
  - What are your initial ideas for the essay? What examples do you think you will need to answer the question well?
  - Make some notes here.
- Step 3: use a method for creating your notes:
  - This could be a mind map or another form of organizer to help you to gather the information you need to write a response to the question.

WRITING AN INTRODUCTION

- Have a look at this sample introduction to the essay question.
- Write down two positives and two criticisms.
- Reflect on how you would develop your own approach to writing an introduction to this question.

> In 1946, Juan Perón was elected into power as the president of Argentina. He had gained popularity due to his position in favour of workers' rights. A variety of economic and political conditions that had been a feature of Argentine history favoured Perón, as he was seen by many to be offering hope to the country, a solution to the troubles of the past.

Positives:

Criticisms:

6 Argentina under Juan Perón, 1946–74

■ Long-term political conditions
- Argentina made some progress in the development of democracy with the **Sáenz Peña electoral reform law** in February 1912.
- The law gave men the right to vote in secret ballots and voting was made compulsory.
- The right to vote was not extended to women and most migrants, who made up a large proportion of the population.
- The political situation saw the growth in political parties and, in particular, gave rise to the **Radical Party** in Argentina, which was elected to power in 1916.

■ Argentina under the Radical Party, 1916–30
- A major challenge to the Radical Party under the presidency of **Hipólito Yrigoyen** was the events of January 1919, known as the 'tragic week' (*la Semana Trágica*).
- A general strike was orchestrated by trade unions, with many of the European migrant workers following the ideas of **syndicalism** and **anarchism**.
- The strike was heavily repressed by the paramilitary group the **Argentine Patriotic League**, leading to a heavy loss of life.
- The social division in Argentina between the trade unionists, as well as continued labour disputes, and the rural **oligarchies** made Argentina difficult to govern during the 1920s. This created tension in the Radical Party over how best to govern the country, leading to splits within the party.
- Yrigoyen's second term in power began in 1928 when he was re-elected as president after the interim presidency of **Marcelo Alvear** (also a member of the Radical Party).
- However, Yrigoyen was ousted in September 1930 by a military coup. The economic problems facing the country were one of the factors that triggered the coup.

■ Short-term economic and political conditions
Following the 1930 military coup, Argentina was controlled by a series of coalition governments known as the **Concordancia**. The years between 1930 and 1943 have become known as the **Decade of Infamy**.

■ The impact of the depression on Argentina
- The economic depression led to a reduced demand for Argentine goods overseas, leading to a sharp decline in their export market. This also led to an unemployment crisis in the country.
- The immediate effects of the depression were one of the factors that led to the overthrow of Yrigoyen's presidency in 1930.
- There were calls for greater levels of autarky within the economy to increase self-sufficiency; nationalists were concerned about the reliance of the Argentine economy on global markets.
- Argentina negotiated a trade deal with Britain in 1933, the **Roca–Runciman Agreement**. This gave the country a fixed share in Britain's beef market. However, it gave British businesses a preferential deal in Argentina, including reduced, unpopular tariffs.
- British privileges over the economy, including British control over trams in Buenos Aires, angered many people.
- There were high levels of rural-to-urban migration during the 1930s, as many rural workers were unable to find work. This increased social division in contrast to the wealth and privilege of the *estancieros*.
- Overall, the depression had the effect of increasing social unrest; it led to increased calls for self-sufficiency and saw the growth of workers' movements looking to protect their interests.

REFLECTING ON SIGNIFICANCE

Reflect on some of the conditions that we have considered so far. Think about why they may be significant to contributing to the uncertain conditions that may have favoured the rise to power of Perón. Use the table below as a template.

Factor	Explanation of significance
Social division in Argentina. Rural elites called *estancieros*. Increased immigration from Europe to Argentina	
Military coups such as September 1930 and political instability (for example, *la Semana Trágica* of 1919)	
Impact of economic depression on Argentina including the unpopularity of the Roca–Runciman Agreement	
Growth and division of political ideas within the country	
Political corruption and rigging elections during Decade of Infamy	

ELIMINATE IRRELEVANCE

- Read the paragraph below and highlight any sections that seem irrelevant to the response in one colour, then highlight any areas which could do with more explanation.
- The paragraph is intended to be an extract from a response to the focus question on page 103.

> Economic conditions were of significance to Perón's rise to power. Argentina had been affected, like many countries (such as Germany), by the economic depression. The depression led to increased unemployment and a restricted international trading market which was a problem for the Argentine export economy. At this point, the USA had introduced the New Deal as a method to manage the economic problems it was experiencing. Further, the depression increased levels of nationalism, especially in relation to the reactions to the Roca–Runciman Agreement of 1933, which was seen to favour British interests.

6 Argentina under Juan Perón, 1946–74

■ The Decade of Infamy

The coup of 1930 that led to the overthrow of Yrigoyen was carried out by the military with the support of the Argentine Patriotic League. There were many different influences on the military at this time, including **fascism** and **corporatism**. This coup led to the beginning of the Decade of Infamy, characterized by corrupt and failing governments, that would last until the second military coup in 1943.

- The Concordancia governments ruled Argentina during the Decade of Infamy. These were an alliance between conservative groups in the country that wanted to help Argentina recover from the depression and often acted in the interests of the rural elites.
- Argentina, compared to other countries at the time, did manage to recover from the depression and make economic progress into the late 1930s.
- During the Decade of Infamy there was also a growth in the size and influence of trade union movements, for example the **General Confederation of Labour (CGT)**, that would later support the policies of Juan Perón.
- Despite some of the economic improvements, the Concordancia governments were politically corrupt, using electoral fraud and repression to maintain their majority rule.

■ The impact of war on Argentina

- Argentina remained neutral for most of the Second World War, as it had in the First World War. There were also groups in Argentina who had a strong connection to Germany at the time, including German migrants. Some German Argentinians served in the military, but there was little support for joining the Axis powers.
- Argentinian neutrality created problems for the USA after the USA went to war with Japan, Germany and Italy. In 1941, the USA passed the **Lend–Lease Act**, which was a commitment of military aid to countries supporting the Allies in the conflict. Given Argentina's neutrality, it received no aid. Other countries in South America did receive military aid, including Brazil, which received the equivalent of $372 million in assistance, a large sum.
- The war also created economic problems for Argentina given the reduced ability to trade during the conflict. This saw reductions in both imports and exports, which increased tension in the country, leading to further demands from nationalists for a more self-sufficient economy.

SOURCE INVESTIGATION

Read the text excerpts below and answer the accompanying questions.

SOURCE 1

Extract from Edwin Williamson, *The Penguin History of Latin America*, Penguin, London, 1992, page 465

The outbreak of the Second World War gave a further impetus to nationalism. Argentina's markets in continental Europe became largely inaccessible, and the flow of imports of technology and fuels needed for her industries was drastically reduced. Nationalists now argued for a policy of state-led industrialization to produce the goods that could no longer be imported and to lessen the economy's reliance on exports.

1. According to Source 1, what were some of the economic consequences for Argentina as a result of the Second World War?

SOURCE 2

Extract from Terence Phelan, 'Behind the Argentine Coup', *Fourth International*, Vol. 4, No. 7, July 1943, pages 209–12 (available at www.marxists.org/history/etol/newspape/fi/vol04/no07/phelan.htm). *Fourth International* was a Marxist magazine that ceased publication in 1956.

Furthermore, parallel with the growth of Allied successes, Argentina has seen itself threatened by increasingly menacing military encirclement. Free Lend–Lease arms, especially planes, have been pouring into the bordering countries, particularly into Brazil. And with them, again particularly into Brazil, were pouring *US* planes, guns, and troops. Meanwhile the US, now the only possible source, refused to sell Argentina any arms whatsoever. Argentina manufactures its own light arms and planes, largely trainers. But it has not in the past manufactured heavy artillery, tanks, and big planes; and even if it now attempted to do so, could not obtain the necessary aluminium and special steels.

2. According to Source 2, how did the actions of the USA negatively affect Argentina during the Second World War?

3. Why is it important to be aware of the Marxist perspective within this source?

SUMMARIZE YOUR UNDERSTANDING

- Take some time to summarize your understanding of the importance of conditions to the rise to power of Perón.
- Using the table below as a template, make sure you have notes on the different conditions. Some examples have been done for you already but try to include more examples within your summary.

Conditions	Examples	Explanation
Social division	Rural-to-urban migration, large population of workers in urban areas	
Economic conditions	Dominance of foreign businesses within the country, including British businesses	
	Disruption of trade due to the economic depression	
Weakness of political system	Corruption within the Concordancia governments	
Impact of war	Disruption of trade due to the Second World War	

6 Argentina under Juan Perón, 1946–74

Methods leading to the rise to power of Perón

The 1943 military coup

An important cause of Perón's rise to power was the military coup in 1943 that brought an end to the Decade of Infamy and the presidency of **Ramón Castillo**. The military coup was carried out by the **United Officers' Group (GOU)** and led to the establishment of a **junta**, with Colonel Juan Perón as a member of the new government.

The role of leaders: Juan Perón

Perón prior to 1943

- Juan Perón, born in 1895, had Italian ancestry and was raised as a Roman Catholic.
- Perón had joined the armed forces at an early age and, by the time of the military coup in 1943, had reached the rank of corporal.
- Perón had travelled to Europe during the late 1930s and early 1940s. He was tasked with studying mountain warfare and observing the governmental systems in Italy and Germany.
- Both Italy and Germany were authoritarian regimes at the time, and it is likely that Perón was influenced by the ideologies of these states, such as the role of corporations in Italy under Benito Mussolini.

Perón after 1943

- Perón was appointed as minister of labour in December 1943. In the previous months he had worked to improve the working conditions of people in the country. A political ally was **Domingo Mercante**, who worked with Perón, in making connections with trade unions and representing their interests.
- An important turning point for Perón's popularity came in the aftermath of the **San Juan earthquake**, which claimed thousands of lives. Perón was a chief organizer of the relief effort. At this time, he met the actress **Eva María Duarte**.
- Shortly after the earthquake, Perón was appointed as vice-president by the new president of the junta, General **Edelmiro Farrell**.
- By early 1944, Perón wielded significant power, holding the office of vice-president and serving as minister of labour.

Explaining Perón's popularity

- Perón's position as a champion of workers' rights increased his popularity.
- As minister of labour, Perón passed a wide variety of legislation that sought to improve workers' conditions, including shorter hours, improved pay and social insurance.
- Perón also did not object to industrial action by unions looking to improve their members' conditions. This position as a supporter of workers led to increasing opposition from other members of the military and political groups who saw him as a threat.
- Perón can be seen as an example of a populist leader, given his concerns for the ordinary working members of society rather than the elites. He was a supporter of social justice, which formed a part of his ideology.

The role of Eva María Duarte

- Perón's popularity was further supported by the efforts of Eva María Duarte, an actress and political activist, also known as Evita. She met Perón at a fundraiser for the victims of the San Juan earthquake.
- Eva set up a range of projects to support workers' rights, including a radio broadcast called **Towards a Better Future**, as well as being an advocate for the **descamisados** (the shirtless ones) in the country, the poorest sections of society.
- Eva played an important role in Perón's release from prison in 1945 and the couple married in December 1945.

The use of force: opposition to Perón

- As mentioned, Perón's promotion of workers' rights led to some opposition within the military and political groups.
- In October 1945, he was asked to resign his position in the government and was arrested and placed in prison.
- Both Eva Duarte and Domingo Mercante played an important role in leading the protests against Perón's arrest and imprisonment. The CGT labour union organization protested.
- Perón was released after four days on 17 October and returned to office. This became known as **Loyalty Day**, celebrating the event and Perón's subsequent ascension to presidency in the months that followed.

Final steps to power

- The events of October 1945 had shown the extent of Perón's popular support.
- He ran for the office of the presidency in February 1946, representing the **Partido Laborista** in the elections.
- His election ticket was opposed by the USA, given Perón's platform which suggested that his rule would be more socialist in nature. This, however, gave Perón further support as he was seen to be campaigning for a more independent and nationalistic Argentina.
- Perón appealed to voters by promising further benefits to workers. Subsequently, he was able to appeal to both the national interest and workers' rights, which gave him the support to win the election. He gained an overwhelming majority in the election and became the new leader of the country.

EXPLAINING PERÓN'S RISE TO POWER

- Alongside the existing conditions in society, Perón's actions in the years between 1943 and 1946 were important to his rise to power.
- Using the table below as a template, explain how each of the following would have contributed to his rise to power and election victory in February 1946.

Perón's actions	Explanation of how it helped in his rise to power
Position in the military, GOU and support for General Edlemiro Farrell	
His position as the minister of labour in the government	
His populist ideology and focus on social justice	
His relationship with Eva Duarte	
His arrest and subsequent release from prison in October 1945	

PERÓN'S IDEOLOGY

SOURCE 3

Extract from Juan Perón's speech called 'What is Perónism?', August 1948, quoted in Juan Perón, *Perónist Doctrine*, Buenos Aires, 1952, page 86 (available at https://library.brown.edu/create/modernlatinamerica/chapters/chapter-9-argentina/primary-documents-w-accompanying-discussion-questions/what-is-peronism-by-juan-domingo-peron-1948-the-twenty-truths-of-the-peronist-justicialism-juan-domingo-peron-1950/).

Perónism is humanism in action; Perónism is a new political doctrine, which rejects all the ills of the politics of previous times; in the social sphere it is a theory which establishes a little equality among men, which grants them similar opportunities and assures them of a future so that in this land there may be no one who lacks what he needs for a living, even though it may be necessary that those who are wildly squandering what they possess may be deprived of the right to do so, for the benefit of those who have nothing at all; in the economic sphere its aim is that every Argentine should pull his weight for the Argentines and that economic policy which maintained that this was a permanent and perfect school of capitalist exploitation should be replaced by a doctrine of social economy under which the distribution of our wealth, which we force the earth to yield up to us and which furthermore we are elaborating, may be shared out fairly among all those who have contributed by their efforts to amass it.

4 According to Source 3, what were some of the features of the Perónist ideology?

_____
_____
_____

5 In what ways does Perón's ideology help to explain his popular support in Argentina?

_____
_____

ESSAY PRACTICE

To practise writing essays on the rise to power of Juan Perón further, attempt one of these essays.

1 Evaluate how the actions of individual leaders have contributed to the emergence of authoritarian states.
2 In what ways have persuasion and coercion been responsible for convincing people to support the creation of authoritarian states?

Perón's domestic policies: aims and results

Methods for the consolidation and maintenance of power

On taking power in 1946, Perón immediately began the process of consolidating his authority and introducing policies designed to bring about his ideological ends.

Consolidating control

- Perón's consolidation of power involved bringing the country's major institutions within his control. These included the army, police, civil service and Roman Catholic Church.
- Perón purged opposition within the army, especially those that had been connected to his previous arrest in October 1945.
- He also used patronage to ensure support. This involved offering incentives to different institutions and individuals to guarantee their backing for his rule. For example, he offered promotion to loyal members of the police force.
- Perón promised the Catholic Church that it would keep its central role in Argentine state and society in return for its support. There were promises that the government would not intervene in the Church's teachings.
- Perón set up the **Partido Perónista** (Perónist Party, also known as the Justicialist Party) early on in his rule, replacing the Labour Party which he had represented in the February 1946 elections.
- The party represented both Perón's authority and ideology.
- From the outset, Perón used authoritarian measures to ensure the stability of his rule. He had dictatorial rights over who could run for election and who was to be in the government, as well being able to overrule political decisions.
- Perón's authority was further strengthened by his control of the media (see page 118).

Controlling the trade unions

- Trade unions were also brought under Perón's control. He closed independent trade unions and replaced them with **syndicates**.
- The CGT, the main workers' organization who had supported Perón's ascendancy, was brought under his control.
- To justify these stricter controls, Perón promised further benefits for workers.
- Opposition to these changes was dealt with harshly. For example, critical union leaders **Cipriano Reyes** and **Luis Gay** were arrested and tortured because of their opposition to Perón's reorganization of the unions.

Economic policies: Perón's first term, 1946–51

A major feature of Perón's first term in office was his policies to develop the economy. He had inherited the economy at a time where it was doing quite well as a result of the Second World War providing a large market for Argentine exports.

Perón's domestic policies: aims and results

ESSAY FOCUS

Let's consider examples of students' work in response to the following question:

Examine the methods used by two authoritarian leaders to consolidate their control.

Both students are looking at the rules of Juan Perón and Adolf Hitler. Pay attention to the annotations to see what is good about their responses and what could be developed.

Student 1

Consolidating control was of importance to both Perón and Hitler. They both used a combination of force and persuasion to align their states around their authority. Perón, for example, made use of the power of patronage to consolidate control. By making assurances to important sources of power in Argentina, he was essentially buying loyalty. Perón made use of patronage with his dealings with the police, the military and the civil service. Further to this, Perón was also willing to use force as required, and opposition to his rule was quickly repressed. Hitler, on the other hand, initially found himself in the position of chancellor, rather than president as was the case for Perón. Hitler's consolidation of power involved using the German Parliament to pass a law, the Enabling Act, which effectively gave him dictatorial powers.

Annotations:
- Point of comparison is made.
- Force and persuasion identified as major factors for consolidation.
- Relevant example identified for explanation.
- The student goes further with the point to add depth to the explanation.
- The example chosen for Hitler is relevant but the explanation could be delivered better. Perhaps needs to explain the situation before the passing of the Enabling Act.

Student 2

Both Hitler and Perón were also keen to reduce the political power of other groups. Perón set up the Perónist Party early on in his rule and made amendments to the constitution which gave him absolute authority. In addition, he sought to closely control the power of the trade unions by bringing them directly under his control. Hitler's first move was to target the Communist Party; after the *Reichstag* Fire, he was able to exercise authority to have the communists all but destroyed as a political force in Germany.

Annotations:
- Comparison point made, placing emphasis on a method of consolidation.
- Example provided but could be developed with a specific example.
- Relevant example to the consolidation of power of Hitler.

Now it's your turn. Practise writing a paragraph on the consolidation of power of Perón and one other authoritarian leader that you are studying. Focus on doing the following things in your response.

- Identifying clearly the method used to consolidate power.
- Providing specific examples to support the points that you are making.
- Making comparison points between the two leaders to demonstrate your understanding.
- Considering the importance or limitation of the method used to show that you are demonstrating your evaluation skills.

Perón's first Five-Year Plan

- Perón introduced a Five-Year Plan which had a range of aims to make the country more self-sufficient, improve working conditions and invest in the country's infrastructure.
- Workers experienced some benefits under the first Five-Year Plan, with wage increases and improved social welfare, including unemployment benefits.
- Nationalization of the central bank, railways, docks and the telephone system.
- Consumer demand for goods increased during the early years of Perón's rule so there were moves to build up the domestic market for goods.
- The **Institute for the Promotion of Argentine Commerce (IAPI)** was established to promote Argentine products.
- Export and imports came under stricter state control, and there were moves to encourage and protect the development of domestic industries in order to reduce the reliance on imports.
- In line with the aim to be independent, Perón decided against joining **GATT** and the **IMF**.

Results

- The Argentine economy did grow in the early years of Perón's rule, but there was some criticism.
- One criticism was over Perón's general approach to policy, which was seen as incoherent. Perón described it as a **Third Way**, which sought to avoid the extremes of communism and capitalism.
- Further, Perón's efforts to become self-sufficient and independent were not sustainable. As countries recovered from the Second World War, there was increasing competition for different markets. The introduction of the **Marshall Plan** by the USA in 1947 was a problem for Perón, as it stimulated multiple economies in the world. Perón's refusal to accept Marshall Aid restricted the country's access to financial assistance at the time.

Economic policies: Perón's second term, 1951–5

Perón was voted in for a second term in 1951 with 64% of the vote, a clear majority. He was still favoured by the people, but during his second term he was to encounter more significant challenges that ended with his overthrow in 1955.

Economic problems

- As mentioned, the country was no longer able to successfully compete in international trade because of the economic recovery stimulated by the Marshall Plan.
- There was more demand for goods than Argentina could produce. As a result, inflation increased, bringing a negative impact on people's savings and leading to a reduction in wages.

The second Five-Year Plan

- The second Five-Year Plan was introduced to address these problems. Perón wanted to encourage agricultural production which could be sold overseas to pay for imports.
- Workers' wages were frozen.
- Foreign investment was allowed. Standard Oil, an American company, was given rights to set up in the south of the country.
- Perón also made the decision to print more money, contributing to inflation and making the Argentinian peso lose value.

Results

- The second Five-Year Plan has been described as a U-turn. This was because of the nature of the economic policies that were more conciliatory towards conservatives and business interests in the country rather than the workers. Perón had moved away from his relationship with the *descamisados*.
- The encouragement of foreign investment was also a different approach from his first term, where the objectives had been focused on greater self-sufficiency.
- Overall, the worsening conditions for people in Argentina during the 1950s increased levels of opposition and created major problems for Perón.

SOURCE INVESTIGATION

SOURCE 4

A poster from 1948 promoting the nationalization of the railways in Argentina ('Perón fulfils: they are now ours!').

6   What is the message of Source 4?
_____
_____

7   How would this type of source help to support Perón's rule?
_____

SOURCE 5

Extract from Bruno Derrick, 'General Perón and the nationalisation of railways in Argentina', *Magazine of The Friends of The National Archives*, Vol. 23, No. 1, April 2012 (available at https://nationalarchives.gov.uk/documents/general-peron.pdf)

In 1948, the government of General Perón nationalised foreign-owned railways in Argentina. Perón, who first took power in 1943 before being elected with a popular mandate in 1945, saw the move as being nationalistic and patriotic. The railways, it was felt, should belong to the 'people'. They had united the country, linking its capital, towns and ports together and enabled trade with Europe and North America. Nationalisation was to have long lasting economic consequences; in the short-term, it abruptly ended the chief outlay for British investment in the country.

8   According to Source 5, why did Perón want to nationalize the railways?
_____
_____

REFLECTING ON SUCCESSES AND FAILURES

- Spend some time consolidating your understanding of Perón's first and second Five-Year Plans.
- Take notes on their aims and relative successes and failures.

Opposition to Perón

Perón sought to consolidate his authority around the Perónist Party and bring different institutions under his control, often through the use of patronage. However, given the worsening conditions during his second presidential term, opposition grew:

- Opposition came from multiple sources. Some explanation of this can be linked to Perón's 'Third Way', which failed to satisfy any of the interest groups entirely.
- The upper classes opposed his measures to improve worker conditions with social reforms. Class division was deeply ingrained in Argentine society. Juan and Eva Perón's close relationship with the *descamisados* was unpopular with the traditional elites.
- On the other side, workers were angered by the strict control of unions, including the CGT. Strikes were illegal, and if they did occur, were often put down ruthlessly by the police. The police were sometimes supported by the extreme right-wing group the **National Liberation Alliance (NLA)**, contributing to a repressive atmosphere.
- This overall opposition increased with the country's worsening economic performance and the impact of inflation on people's prosperity.
- It is worth noting that following the death of Eva Perón in 1952, opposition increased to her husband's rule. Given her popularity, she in many ways was the figurehead of Perónism for the people.

Opposition from the Roman Catholic Church

- A major conflict during Perón's second term was with the Catholic Church. In his first term he had made assurances about the Church's independence and importance for moral guidance to the nation.
- Church leaders became increasingly critical of Perón's rule, especially his personality cult that was exaggerated by propaganda.
- Perón's social policies had aggravated the Church, including the legalization of divorce and prostitution. Perón's character was called into question by Church leaders.
- Tension increased with Perón's attempt to outlaw the Christian Democrat political party that represented the Church, as well as his expulsion of two bishops from the country. The Catholic Church reacted strongly to Perón's actions and he was **excommunicated** in 1955.
- A Perónist rally at the **Plaza de Mayo** in Buenos Aires on 16 June 1955 was attacked by a section of the air force, killing over 350 people.
- Perónists responded strongly by attacking churches, with violence breaking out in the streets of Buenos Aires.
- Perón called for a **5:1 ratio**, saying that five opponents should be killed for every one Perónist killed.
- The situation escalated, leading to a military coup in September 1955.

Opposition from the military

- Perón was overthrown by discontented military leaders in September 1955. Perón's moves against the Church had alienated many.
- Perón had never been able to count fully on the support of the entire military given the different factions that existed. His increasing loss of control had convinced some to rise up against him. The coup was led by General **Eduardo Lonardi**.
- Perón was able to escape to Paraguay, where he would remain in exile until his return to power in 1973.

Perón's domestic policies: aims and results

PERÓN'S OVERTHROW, 1955

In 1955, Perón was ousted from power. He lived in Paraguay until 1973. Practise writing an extended response to explain the reasons for Perón's loss of power in 1955. You should try to include the five points provided in the box to give your response some structure and supporting evidence. The sentence starters have been done for you.

> By September 1955, Perón's second term in office had ended with him being overthrown by the military. The situation for Perón had been slipping out of his control from some time, for example the economy …
>
> Alongside these economic policies, there were increasing levels of dissatisfaction in society coming from both richer and poorer people. Perón's 'Third Way' political position, although attempting to bring the country together, was …
>
> Perón had also suffered the loss of his wife Eva in 1952. This was a major loss to him as well as to the movement …
>
> However, the conflict which brought Perón's rule to an end can be seen in his relations with the Roman Catholic Church …

- Economic problems connected with rising inflation.
- The death of Eva Perón.
- Perón's 'Third Way'.
- Conflict with the Roman Catholic Church.
- Opposition from the military.

SOURCE ANALYSIS

SOURCE 6

Extract from Eva Perón's speech to *descamisados* on 17 October 1951 (available at www.marxists.org/history/argentina/peron/1951/speech.htm).

Let the enemies of the people, of Perón and the Fatherland come. I have never been afraid of them because I have always believed in the people. I have always believed in my beloved *descamisados* because I have never forgotten that without them October 17 would have been a date of pain and bitterness, for this date was supposed to be one of ignominy and treason, but the courage of this people turned it into a day of glory and happiness. Finally, compañeros [companions], I thank you for all your prayers for my health; I thank you with all my heart. I hope that God hears the humble of my Fatherland so that I can quickly return to the struggle and be able to keep on fighting with Perón for you and with you for Perón until death. I don't ask or want anything for myself. My glory is and always will be to be Perón's shield and the flag of my people, and though I leave shreds of my life along the road, I know that you will pick up my name and will carry it to victory as a banner. I know that God is with us because he is with the humble and despises the arrogance of the oligarchy. This is why victory will be ours. We will achieve it sooner or later, whatever the cost, whoever may fall.

9   Read through the extract in Source 6. How does it help you to understand:
   a   Eva Perón's popular appeal?
   b   The ideology of Perónism?
   c   The use of propaganda by the Peróns?

Argentina, 1955–73

- After the 1955 coup, Perón would remain out of Argentina until 1973. During this time there were a variety of governments who inherited the political structure and economic legacy of Perón's rule. All of these governments struggled to bring stability to the country.
- Perón's influence remained very strong within Argentina during his absence as he still had the support of the CGT, as well as those Perónists who had continued to support him during the conflict with the Church. He cultivated connections with different political leaders during his exile, such as Ernesto 'Che' Guevara, to whom he paid tribute on his death in 1967 (see Source 7).
- Perónism as a movement fragmented during this time, with the development of a more radical left-wing group, the **Montoneros**, who were committed to extreme methods, such as kidnapping and murdering former President **Pedro Aramburu** in 1970 for his involvement in the 1955 coup.
- With increasing calls for democratic reform in the country, Perón, with support from the army, was able to return to Argentina in June 1973 to make his final bid for power.

SOURCE 7

Juan Perón's tribute to Ernesto 'Che' Guevara on hearing of his death in 1967, quoted in Kerry Bolton, *Perón and Perónism*, Black House Publishing, London, 2014, page 320.

His life, his epic – is the clearest example to our young people, young people throughout Latin America.

There will always be those who will attempt to tarnish his name. Imperialism has a huge fear of charisma, and he managed to win the hearts of the masses of our subjugated people. Already I have received news that the Argentine Communist Party, has begun a hypocritical smear campaign to discredit him. This is not surprising, because it was always known that they act contrary to the historical national interest. They were always against the national and popular movements. We Peronists can attest to that.

Perón's third term, 1973–4

- In March 1973, **Héctor Cámpora** was elected president of Argentina; he was a left-wing Perónist.
- Juan Perón was now able to return to Argentina and arrived at Buenos Aires airport in June, alongside Cámpora.
- However, Perón's return to the country was marked by conflict between the different factions of Perónists.
- In the **Ezeiza massacre**, shots were fired into a crowd of Montoneros and the **Perónist Youth**, leading to a number of deaths.
- Within a few months, Perón was elected into office for the third time, alongside his wife **Isabel Martínez de Perón**, who would serve as vice-president.
- Perón's economic policies were similar to those of his first term. He nationalized banks, prioritized local businesses, offering them subsidies, and passed measures to provide more social security to workers.
- Alongside economic policy, he sought to end the division within the movement, repressing the left wing, specifically the Montoneros.
- Right-wing Perónist **José López Rega** led this movement against the left. The **Triple A**, the Argentine Anti-Communist Alliance, was also used to destroy the left opposition.
- Perón died in July 1974 having failed to bring about national unity. His widow Isabel took over as the new president of Argentina after his death.

Perón's domestic policies: aims and results

SOURCE INVESTIGATION

During Perón's absence from Argentina, the Perónist movement continued, looking forward to the return of its leader. The movement also split into different branches. An active group in the 1960s and early 1970s was the military and revolutionary wings, the Montoneros. Consider the sources and answer the questions.

10 Using Source 7 on the previous page, what does it suggest about Juan Perón's relationship with revolutionaries and his ideology during the 1960s?

SOURCE 8

Photograph of the Montoneros in Argentina in 1972, a more militant left-wing branch of Perónism.

SOURCE 9

Extract from Mitchell Abidor, 'The Montoneros' (available at www.marxists.org/history/argentina/montoneros/introduction.htm).

In their early days their primary demand was for the return of Peron to both Argentina and power (*Peron Vuelve!*) and an end to the illegitimate governments that had succeeded him. The Montonero's entry onto the Argentine political scene was signaled in striking fashion, with the June 1, 1970 kidnapping and execution of the former president of Argentina General Pedro Aramburu. Their almost Christ-like veneration of the Perons was one of the motive forces for the kidnapping and killing of the General. In their communiqué announcing the kidnapping they enumerated the charges against Aramburu, which included 'the public defamation of the names of the legitimate popular leaders in general and especially of our leader Juan Domingo Peron,' as well as 'the profanation of the place where the remains of Compañera Evita were resting and the later disappearance of same, taking from the people even the final material remains of she who was their standard bearer.' Such loyalty could not but please Peron, who saw the Montoneros and their violence as a key element in his strategy for return to power.

12 According to Source 9, what were the aims of the Montoneros?

11 What information does Source 8 give you about the Montoneros?

13 In what ways were the Montoneros important for Perón's return to power?

SOURCE 10

Extract from Michael Lynch, *Access to History for the IB Diploma: Authoritarian states*, second edition, Hodder Education, London, 2015, page 285.

His [Perón's] greatest problem was the deep division between his followers. During his eighteen-year absence, the Left-Wing of the Perónist groupings, the *montoneros*, had become a predominant element. They had supported Perón's return in the belief that he would crush both the conservatives and trade unionists and turn Argentina into a fully socialist society. But Perón resolved instead to crush the *montoneros*. Backed by the moderates and conservatives in the army and the party, he authorized extra-legal measures to be used against them.

14 What does Source 10 suggest about Perón's political stance once he had returned to power in 1973?

Life in Argentina under the rule of Perón

The extent of authoritarian control

Although Perón's rule over Argentina could not be described as totalitarian, when examining the nature of the Perónist state one can find plenty of evidence of a high level of authoritarian control.

Controlling the media and Perón's cult of personality
- The media were strictly controlled from early on. Different media outlets, such as newspapers and radio, were expected to promote Perón's government and criticism was not tolerated. This was enforced by the **Descato Law**.
- The national daily newspaper *La Prensa* came under Perónist control after it was taken over by the CGT.
- The media were also used to promote the cult of personality of both Juan and Eva Perón.
- Their images could be found everywhere, reinforcing their authority over the country and adding to their populist appeal.

Control of the courts
- The legal system and the courts were also closely controlled under Perón.
- Perón was keen to have his supporters working in the courts and would dismiss those who were against him.
- He replaced the members of the Supreme Court with his supporters after they had resisted his policies.

Control of academics and the arts
- Universities were closely monitored, with dissident departments being closed down or having their funding cut.
- There was an exodus of academics from the country under Perón due to the restricted freedoms including the censorship of publications.
- Those working in the arts faced similar difficulties, with censorship being used against critics of the regime.
- There were a number of examples of people working in the arts who came under close scrutiny from Perón, including comic actress **Niní Marshall**, pianist **Osvaldo Pugliese** and film director **Luis Saslavsky**.
- Better-known opposition could be seen in the work and life of the writer and public figure **Jorge Luis Borges**. He became president of the **Society of Argentinian Writers (SADE)**, an organization committed to free speech. Borges regularly spoke out against the Peróns, viewing them as corrupt dictators who were bad for the country.

Control of education
- Schools were expected to support the rule of Juan Perón, with an emphasis on promoting his speeches and writing, as well as those of his wife.
- The cult of personality was reinforced with deferential references to the leaders, with Juan Perón being known as the **Liberator of the People** and Eva Perón as the **Spiritual Chief of the Nation**.
- Schools were expected to teach aspects of the Perónist ideology, namely *justicialismo*, and its importance to the country.
- Education was a main source of conflict with the Roman Catholic Church. After initially promising to uphold the role of the Church within education, Perón started to introduce measures that looked to curtail its influence during his second term.
- These measures included the removal of religious teaching, cutting funding to Roman Catholic schools and the abolition of the **Department of Religious Teaching**.

Life in Argentina under the rule of Perón

SPIDER DIAGRAM

Using the template below, create a spider diagram showing the different ways that Juan Perón set about controlling the state. You can use the information on the opposite page to help you, as well as the previous sections that examined how he used patronage to gather support from the institutions of the state.

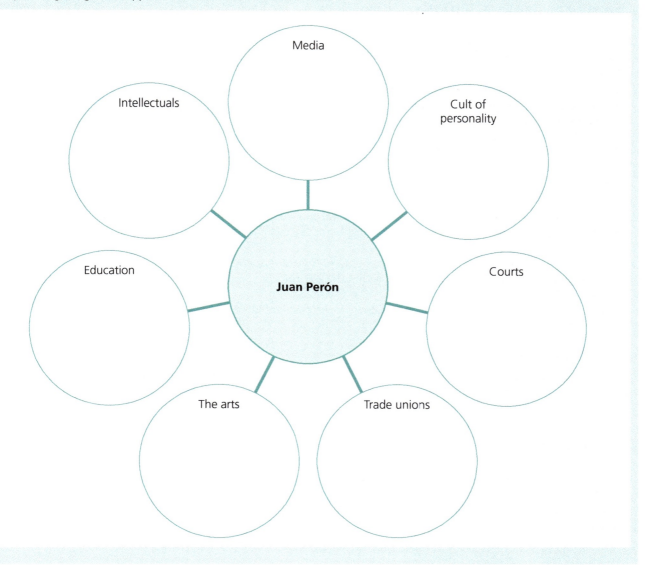

SOURCE ANALYSIS

Look at the official portrait of Juan and Eva Perón, painted in 1948 by Numa Ayrinhac, at the following address:
https://upload.wikimedia.org/wikipedia/commons/f/f3/Museo_del_Bicentenario_-_%22Retrato_de_Juan_Domingo_Per%C3%B3n_y_Eva_Duarte%22%2C_Numa_Ayrinhac.jpg

15 How does the official portrait of the Peróns in 1948 reinforce the following:
   a The cult of personality?
   _____
   b Nationalism?
   _____
   c Gender roles?
   _____

Treatment of minorities

When compared to other authoritarian rulers of the twentieth century, Perón's treatment of minorities seems to be one of promoting tolerance; his commitments to social justice, in theory, extended to all people in the country. However, his attitudes towards same-sex relationships and accusations of connections to Nazi Germany during the 1940s call for closer examination.

Treatment of gay/lesbian people
- Homosexual activity had been decriminalized in Argentina in the late nineteenth century.
- There is limited evidence of persecution of gay/lesbian people under Perón's rule.
- However, there are suggestions that Perón wanted to celebrate and encourage heterosexual relationships, so he promoted the tango, the traditional Argentine dance which reinforced heterosexual gender roles.
- A 2016 book by Nicolás Márquez called *Perón: El Fetiche de las Masas* (*Perón: The Fetish of the Masses*) suggests that Perón was intolerant and that he tried to ban gay/lesbian people from voting in Argentina.

Treatment of Jewish people
- A major criticism of Perón and his rule was the suspicion and allegations of sympathizing with the Nazi regime and providing a safe haven for escaping Nazis, including **Adolf Eichmann** and **Josef Mengele**.
- There were, however, no policies of discrimination towards Jewish people. Jewish people were provided with equal rights and many worked within the government system and acted as advisers to Perón.
- Further, Argentina gave formal recognition to Israel in 1948 and developed good relations with the country under Perón.

Treatment of minority ethnic groups
- There were no policies to promote racial discrimination during Perón's rule. His focus on the *decamisados*, the poorest members of society, incorporated minority groups, including those of Native American descent. However, it can be observed that there was lack of specific policies to help minority ethnic groups in the country.

Role and status of women

The lives of women in Argentina were supported by the policies of Perón, especially as seen in the work of Eva Perón. Her experiences of poverty early on in life, as well as her prominence as a celebrity, allowed her to carry out numerous roles designed to improve the lives of people in the country. Overall, the status of women was that of a progression towards a more equal society and there were moves to improve the conditions for women throughout Argentina:

- An early move was to grant women the vote in 1947; this was celebrated very publicly, adding to the charismatic appeal of Juan and Eva Perón.
- Eva Perón, with the support of her husband, set up the **Women's Perónist Political Party** in 1947, which sought to give a voice to women. Its membership grew rapidly with branches across the country.
- She also set up the **Eva Perón Foundation**, an institution committed to social welfare which carried out numerous projects in the fields of education and health and improving working conditions.
- Thousands of schools were established by the foundation, as well as kindergartens for young children. Health centres were set up with a focus on elderly care. Workers were provided with holiday resorts. A coastal theme park, the **Republic of the Children**, was set up in 1951 to provide entertainment for younger people.
- By the early 1950s, there had been a range of improvements affecting the lives of women. As well as the vote, the number of women in employment increased, as did the number attending university. Women were also represented in the high branches of Argentine government in the Congress and Senate.
- After the death of Eva Perón in 1952, the pace of reform slowed and the remaining years of Juan Perón's rule did not demonstrate the same commitments as seen previously.

COMPARE AND CONTRAST

Compare and contrast the status and treatment of women and minorities in two authoritarian states.

Using Juan Perón and one other authoritarian leader, attempt to write a response to this question. You could use this essay plan template to help your answer. These are just some ideas to get you to think about how to structure your writing.

- Introduction: introduce the question and provide a thesis, which is a short explanation of your overall response to the question. You may want to put some introductory information here about the two states that you have chosen.
- Section 1: compare the status and treatment of women. Write a paragraph or paragraphs about the ways that the two states held similarities. Think about the different aims for women in society as well as outcomes. Consider whether both authoritarian states brought progress to women's rights.
- Section 2: contrast the status and treatment of women. Write a paragraph or paragraphs about the different approaches to policies towards women. One state may have done much more to advance women's rights (or reverse rights). For Perón, the role of Eva Perón should be considered – showing the importance of individuals.
- Section 3: compare the status and treatment of minorities. Think about whether the two states were progressive or inclusive of minorities. Were there any contradictions? In this section write up some comparison points.
- Section 4: contrast the status and treatment of minorities. Finally, consider the different experiences of minority groups in the two states. There will probably be a range of points to consider here.
- Conclusion: reach an overall response to the question. Try to reflect on the nature of the authoritarian states in the question. Consider whether their ideology was put into practice. Think about how people's lives changed overall as a result.

REVIEW QUESTIONS

Check your understanding of Juan Perón's rule by going through the following review questions:

1. What were the social and economic conditions in Argentina at the start of the twentieth century?
2. What examples are there of political instability prior to the coup of 1943?
3. How did the Second World War impact Argentina?
4. How did Juan Perón appeal to the workers in Argentina in the years before the 1946 presidential election?
5. How would you describe Perón's ideology? Why is it difficult to define?
6. What were the main features of Perón's economic policies?
7. What methods were used to consolidate Perón's control over Argentina?
8. What opposition existed to Perón's rule?
9. Why was Perón overthrown in 1955?
10. Explain the conditions in Argentina during Perón's exile. Why was he able to return to power in 1973?
11. How did Perón's relationship with the Catholic Church change during his rule?
12. How did the lives of women change under the rule of Perón?
13. What was the significance of Eva Perón to Argentine society?

Exam focus

Sample question and answer

Consider the response to the essay question below. Pay attention to the annotations and overall comment.

Examine the ways in which authoritarian rule was maintained in one state.

Juan Perón's rule in Argentina during the middle part of the twentieth century changed the experiences of the country in many ways. Placing himself as an advocate of a Third Way in terms of ideology and policy, Perón has defied convention in terms of political labelling. Perón can definitely be described as a populist ruler, especially given his focus on the workers who came out in their masses to support him on 17 October 1945, leading to his release from prison and subsequent rise to power. Perón served three terms as president of Argentina and his methods to retain power were varied. What can be concluded is that he retained an authority over the country, even during his exile, which was brought about by a combination of popular policies and authoritarian control.

On winning the presidential election in February 1946, Perón sought to consolidate his authority over the country. By setting up the Perónist political party, using patronage to encourage loyalty across the different branches of government and taking control of the media, he quickly put himself into a strong position. The media were used effectively to promote his policies and speeches; criticism was not tolerated. Perón's ideology was promoted to the people through speeches as well as through the development of a cult of personality both around him as leader and around his wife Eva Perón, who was a favourite of the *descamisado*, the 'shirtless ones', the poorest sectors of Argentine society. Speeches by both Juan and Eva were used to promote the movement, for example the 'Twenty Truths' speech which talked about the importance of a range of concepts including national unity, social justice and welfare.

Economic policies were also used to maintain rule over Argentina, but here there was more inconsistency in terms of results. The economic policies of Perón's first term in office brought a range of benefits to the country. There was a lot of national pride over the nationalization of industries including the railways. In addition, investment in workers led to some improvements including increases in wages and unemployment benefits. However, due to a variety of factors, the economic performance slowed down into the second term of Perón's presidency and there was rising inflation. Economic policies by the 1950s moved to a more conservative platform with wage freezes for workers as well as encouraging foreign investment in the country. The economy therefore, as has been the case for many leaders in Argentina in the past, represented both an opportunity and a challenge to Perón. With the worsening economic conditions during the 1950s, he was increasingly having to move away from his original principles and increase the levels of repression in society due to mounting opposition.

Therefore, a significant method of control was through the use of authoritarianism. Perón brought in controls that sought to reduce, if not silence, opposition. For example, artists and intellectuals were monitored under Perón. Given the repressive atmosphere, numerous people migrated from Argentina because of this. Education was used to reinforce Perónist values and the authority of the rulers. Picture books showing Juan

Annotations:
- Good awareness of context surrounding Perón.
- Thesis provided, shows the line of argument for the essay.
- Range of supporting evidence here.
- Use of key terminology.
- Explanation and understanding demonstrated.
- Comparison to other aspects of history.
- Connective for the next paragraph.

and Eva as the patriarch and matriarch of the nation reinforced their cult of personality. However, Perón never had 'total' control over the country, as seen in 1955 when he was overthrown by a military coup. The coup was largely caused by Perón's conflicts with the Roman Catholic Church but was carried out by the military. This suggests that Perón's methods to maintain his authority over Argentina were dependent on certain factors that were not fully under his control.

> Evaluation provided.

Although Perón was not ruling Argentina between 1955 and 1973, it is important to note that his influence lived on through the political climate of the time. This suggests that the legacy of Perón was the ideological movement that inspired many people in the country. Perónism continued to be a political force, and the movement split into different factions. A notable group was the Montoneros, a military and revolutionary wing of the party that wanted to bring their exiled leader back into prominence. This was achieved towards the end of 1973, and Perón began his third term as president. However, analysis of this third term in connection with his maintenance of power is challenging due to its brief time span and his failing health. What we do see though is Perón's use of force to maintain power. Through the actions of the Triple A and the influence of José López Rega we see an increasingly violent repression of the socialist aspects of the movement which continued after his death.

> Relevant supporting evidence.

In conclusion, Perón's maintenance of power was based on authoritarian control and populist appeal. He was able to win the support of the people through his appeal and policies that sought to bring about more *justicialismo* to society. This was particularly evident in the work of his wife Eva Perón. However, there were also high levels of authoritarian control to reduce opposition and maintain his cult of personality. Perón's continued popularity during his exile showed the tremendous effect he had on the country and his legacy lives on to this day. Interpreting and appraising Perón's impact on Argentina is challenging given the complexities of both the political situation at the time and the contradictions throughout his rule.

> Goes further, shows challenges of answering the question in this context.

A well-written response that demonstrates a synthesis of evidence to develop a line of argument. There is an evaluation of arguments and a good historical awareness throughout the essay. The essay has structure and considers a range of points in connection to Perón's maintenance of power. The conclusion argues consistently with the evidence presented and mentions challenges associated with the study of Perón.

Exam practice

Now either have a go at the above essay question or try one of the following questions, with reference to Perón's Argentina:

1 Compare and contrast the role of charismatic leadership for the maintenance of power in two authoritarian states.

2 'Economic problems and social division create the ideal conditions for the emergence of authoritarian states.' Discuss whether you agree with this statement with reference to two authoritarian states.

3 Examine the successes and failures of cultural policies in one authoritarian state.

Glossary

1868–79 Wars of Independence Series of conflicts between Cuban independence movements and the Spanish.

1905 Revolution Protests against the rule of Tsar Nicholas II, which led to creation of the *Duma*.

1922 Moscow Trial of the Socialist Revolutionaries Example of a show trial carried out under Lenin.

1936 Family Code Soviet decree which included outlawing abortion, made divorce more difficult to obtain and encouraged an increase in the birth rate.

1975 Family Code Provided details on the rights of people in Cuba concerning marriage, divorce and having children.

21 Demands Issued by Japan during the First World War to gain more economic control over areas of China.

25-Point Programme Published in the early 1920s, this was the early ideology of the Nazi Party.

26 July Movement Name given to the movement that was aiming to overthrow Batista.

28 Bolsheviks Members of the Chinese Communist Party who had received training in Moscow.

5:1 Ratio Term used by Perón to demand the deaths of five people for every one Perónist killed in the unrest of 1955.

Agitprop Political propaganda, usually through the medium of arts.

Amnesty Giving an official pardon or freedom to someone who has been convicted.

Anarchism Ideology which seeks to remove organized forms of governance.

Anschluss The union of Germany and Austria in 1938.

Anti-Campaigns Reform movements in China to get rid of different things in society, for example corruption. The Three and Five Anti-Campaigns were examples of this.

Anti-Comintern Pact Signed between Germany and Japan in 1936 against the USSR.

Anti-Rightist Campaign A response to the Hundred Flowers Campaign where critics of the Chinese Communist Party were arrested and imprisoned.

April Theses A series of demands made by Lenin in April 1917 that laid out the priorities for the revolution and creation of a new socialist state.

Argentine Patriotic League Paramilitary group that was strongly anti-communist.

Article 231 The war guilt clause of the Treaty of Versailles.

Article 48 Article of the Weimar constitution that allowed the president 'emergency powers' in times of crisis.

Aryans People of northern European racial descent, held up as the 'master race' by the Nazis.

Austerity Conditions introduced by a government during difficult economic conditions, involving less public expenditure.

Autarky Meaning self-sufficient, a central aim of Nazi economic policy.

Autobahn A high-speed road in Germany. Some were built during the public works schemes of the 1930s.

Autumn Harvest Uprising Uprising led by Mao against the Guomindang in Hunan and Jiangxi provinces, which took place in 1927.

Backyard steel furnaces Makeshift techniques for producing steel by the Chinese people during the Great Leap Forward.

Balance of trade The difference between imports and exports.

Battle of La Plata Military victory for the Cuban 26 July Movement in July 1958.

Battle of Tannenburg First World War battle of August 1914 involving heavy Russian casualties.

Bay of Pigs The site of a failed CIA-backed attempt by Cuban émigrés to retake Cuba from Castro.

Black Cubans Cubans of African descent; also those who have connections to Haiti and the West Indies.

Black Spring A wave of arrests of dissidents in Cuba in 2003.

Bolshevik Party Political party based on Marxist ideas, led by Lenin.

Bolshevik Revolution Overthrow of the Provisional Government in October 1917, eventually leading to the creation of the USSR.

Brain drain When large numbers of skilled people leave a country, causing problems for employment.

Capitalist roader Mao's term for someone who tried to promote capitalism in China.

Catholic Centre Party (*Zentrum*) Large political party during the Weimar era, which voted in support of the Enabling Act in 1933.

Cheka Secret police under Lenin.

Chinese Civil War Conflict between the Chinese Communist Party and Guomindang, 1946–9.

Chinese Communist Party (CCP) The founding and ruling party of the People's Republic of China.

CIA Central Intelligence Agency, a US government organization, founded in 1947, to gather information and carry out surveillance outside the USA. Has been involved in paramilitary activities.

Collective security An international relations' effort which seeks to increase security by working together to form defensive pacts and alliances.

Collectivization Agricultural policy of grouping farms together to create large state farms.

Comintern International organization set up by Lenin in the early 1920s for spreading communist ideas around the world.

Committee for the Defence of the Revolution (CDR) Local committees in Cuba for people to build community, but also used to maintain conformity and compliance with the Communist Party.

Communes Set up in China to help with collectivization and industrialization from 1958; involved the grouping together of thousands of households to work and live collectively.

Communist Party (KPD) Significant political party during the Weimar era; had links with the USSR and was forced underground after Hitler took power in 1933.

Communist Party of the Soviet Union (CPSU) Official title of the Soviet Communist Party.

Concentration camps Prison facilities run by the SS that were used to hold people, for example at Dachau. The Nazis also set up death camps which were used to carry out the Holocaust.

Concordancia Name given to the Argentine coalition governments during the 'Decade of Infamy'.

Confessional Church Protestant opposition movement to the Nazis' plans to unify the churches under their leadership and ideology.

Confucianism Traditional Chinese philosophy which emphasized hierarchy, tradition and social harmony.

Contras US-backed militias who worked in Nicaragua to try to overthrow the Sandinistas.

Corporatism Giving power to large corporations within a system of government.

Council of Ministers Highest branch of government in Cuba, set up after Fidel Castro took power.

Council of People's Commissars Government institution of the USSR.

Cuban émigrés Cubans who left the island after Castro took power. A number of the émigrés were involved in the Bay of Pigs invasion.

Cuban Missile Crisis Major Cold War stand-off between the USA and the USSR after mid-range nuclear missiles were deployed in Cuba.

Cuban Revolution The event that brought Fidel Castro and the 26 July Movement to power in 1959.

Cuban Women's Federation (FMC) Organization that represented women's interests in Cuba; also carried out various projects and policies directed at helping women to gain skills and employment.

Cultural Revolution The time in China, between 1966 and 1976, when Mao's authority was promoted, the 'four olds' were attacked and the Red Guards caused chaos.

Dachau The first concentration camp set up under the Nazis, opened in March 1933.

Decade of Infamy Used to describe the series of governments in Argentina between 1930 and 1943 which were politically corrupt.

De-kulakization The Soviet policy against the kulaks that involved the arrest, deportation and execution of millions of *kulaks*.

Democratic centralism Advocated by Lenin; reinforced the importance of a central body of decision-makers having absolute authority.

Denunciation Speaking out against someone in a local area.

Department of Religious Teaching Set up to oversee religious teaching in Argentina, later disbanded by Perón during his conflict with the Roman Catholic Church.

Der Stürmer A newspaper in Germany that supported the policies of the Nazi Party.

Descamisados The 'shirtless ones'; refers to the poorest sections of Argentine society.

Descato Law Meaning contempt, a law passed by Juan Perón which called for conformity in the media.

Diktat Dictated peace, an expression used to describe the Treaty of Versailles.

Diversification In Cuba, this referred to the attempts to develop a range of industries to reduce dependency on the sugar trade.

Doctors' Plot Towards the end of Stalin's rule, this event was an accusation of a number of senior doctors in Moscow stating that they planned to assassinate leading members of the party.

Duma The Russian assembly that functioned between 1906 and 1917.

Edelweiss Pirates Youth group which sought to be free from state interference and oppose the Nazis.

El Cubano Libre *The Free Cuban*: a publication set up by Guevara to promote the work of the 26 July Movement.

Emancipation of the Serfs 1861 decree by Tsar Alexander II that gave freedom to the serfs (agricultural labourers), including the promise of land ownership.

Enabling Act Law passed by the *Reichstag* in March 1933 that effectively gave Hitler dictatorial powers.

Glossary

Ersatz goods Replacement goods that were made domestically to reduce the reliance on imports. Usually of a poorer quality.

Escambray Area of central Cuba.

Estancieros The rich rural owners of estates in Argentina.

Eternal Jew, The A Nazi anti-Semitic film made in 1940.

Ethnic cleansing The mass deportation or killing of an ethnic group in an area.

Eugenics A racial pseudoscience that was taught in Nazi schools to promote Aryan supremacy; it was also used as the justification for policies such as forced sterilization in Germany during the 1930s.

Eva Perón Foundation Set up to help impoverished people, and develop Argentine education and health services.

Excommunicated Officially excluded from the Roman Catholic Church.

Ezeiza massacre Incident at the Ezeiza airport in Buenos Aires in 1973 when right-wing factions fired on the Montoneros and the Perónist Youth as they were gathering to welcome the return of Juan Perón to Argentina.

Factionalism Process of creating divisions within a political party based on differences of opinion on ideology and policy.

Fascism Authoritarian and nationalistic political ideology of the twentieth century, observed in Italy under the rule of Benito Mussolini.

February Revolution Russian revolution in 1917 that led to the abdication of Tsar Nicholas II.

First Sino-Japanese War War between China and Japan in 1894–5.

Five-Year Plan Economic targets and plans – used by the USSR and the PRC.

Four-Year Plan Göring's economic policies for Nazi Germany that included rearmament and the development of domestic goods to reduce the reliance on imports.

French invasion of the Ruhr Invasion of the industrial Ruhr region in Germany by French and Belgian soldiers in 1923 in response to Germany's failure to keep up with reparations payments.

Führer Meaning leader; title given to Hitler after 1934.

Functionalist Historiographical tradition that emphasizes systems and the people working within them who play a major role on effecting change in societies.

Futian Incident A mutiny by Red Army soldiers against Mao's leadership that was met with fierce repression.

Gang of Four Four members of the Chinese Communist Party who promoted the Cultural Revolution. The gang included Jiang Qing (Mao's wife).

GATT General Agreement on Tariffs and Trade; agreed in 1948 to promote international trade.

General Confederation of Labour (CGT) National trade union federation in Argentina; formed in 1930.

German Labour Front (DAF) National trade union set up for all workers in Germany; independent trade unions were prohibited.

German National People's Party (DNVP) Major conservative political party during the Weimar era.

German People's Party (DVP) Liberal political party during the Weimar era.

German Workers' Party (DAP) Forerunner of the NSDAP, founded by Anton Drexler. Adolf Hitler was also a member of this party, which was in existence from 1919 to 1920.

Gestapo German secret police during the rule of the Nazis.

Gleichschaltung The process of bringing different systems and institutions under the control of the Nazis, for example the outlawing of other political parties.

Golden Age of Weimar The improved period of Weimar 1924–9, which included better economic conditions and a range of cultural developments.

Grand Alliance The Second World War alliance of the UK, the USSR and the USA.

Granma **expedition** Named after the yacht that took members of 26 July Movement from Mexico to Cuba in 1956. The trip encountered numerous difficulties.

Great Leap Forward The second Five-Year Plan in China, which involved the creation of communes and high industrial targets. It is largely regarded as a disaster for the country.

Great Retreat Label given to Stalin's social policy for the reversal of many of Lenin's policies concerning women and education.

Great Terror The escalation of political purges in the USSR, 1936–8. Targets included the peasantry, military officers and members of the party. Hundreds of thousands of people died during this time.

Guajiros Rural workers in Cuba.

Guantánamo Bay An area of Cuba leased by the USA after the Spanish–American War.

Guerrilla A fighter who uses unconventional military tactics in combat.

Guerrilla warfare Military strategy that involves irregular and unpredictable techniques, often making use of natural environments.

Gulag A Soviet prison camp.

Gulag Archipelago, The A book written by Alexander Solzhenitsyn, first published in 1973, that discusses the nature of the *gulag* system in the USSR.

Guns or Butter The debate over the direction of the German economy: focus on consumer goods or rearmament?

Guomindang (GMD) The Nationalist Party in China originally led by Sun Yat-sen.

Han The major ethnic group in China.

History will absolve me The speech that Castro made at his trial after being arrested for his involvement in the Moncada Barracks attack.

Hitler Youth A youth organization of the Nazi Party.

Holocaust Mass murder of Jewish people in Europe by the Nazis, carried out in death camps and concentration camps. Around 6 million Jewish people were killed.

Holy See The administration of the Catholic Church based in Vatican City, which represents the whole Church.

Hujum Policy by the Communist Party of the Soviet Union to discourage Muslim women from wearing veils.

Hyperinflation Severe economic conditions leading to very high monetary inflation.

Ideologue Someone committed to a specific ideology.

IMF International Monetary Fund; formed in 1945 to stabilize international financial markets and promote international trade.

Individualism Referring to the needs or rights of individuals.

Industrialization Process of increasing industrial output in a country.

Institute for the Promotion of Argentine Commerce (IAPI) Set up by Perón to promote the development of domestic industries in Argentina.

Institute of Agrarian Reform Organization set up in 1959 to oversee land reform in Cuba.

Intentionalism Historiographical tradition that emphasizes the role of individuals in shaping events in history.

Jiangxi Soviet An area under Chinese Communist Party control, 1927–34. The area was repeatedly attacked by Chiang during the Encirclement Campaigns.

July Bomb Plot A failed assassination attempt on Adolf Hitler, led by Colonel Claus von Stauffenberg, on 20 July 1944.

Junta A military government, particularly in a Spanish- or Portuguese-speaking country.

Kadets A liberal Russian political party. Its formal name was the Constitutional Democratic Party.

Kapp *Putsch* Attempted overthrow of the Weimar Republic, led by Wolfgang Kapp, in March 1920.

Kinder, Küche, Kirche A German slogan meaning 'children, kitchen, church' used derogatorily to describe women's roles.

Kolkhoz A collective farm in the USSR.

Korean War Conflict between North and South Korea, 1950–3.

Kreisau Circle An opposition group to Hitler and the Nazi state; it met in the home of its leader, Helmuth von Moltke, to discuss its plans.

Kristallnacht Series of attacks on Jewish businesses and buildings in Germany in 1938.

Kronstadt Rebellion Uprising against the Bolsheviks in 1921, it led to the introduction of the New Economic Policy.

Kulaks 'Affluent' agricultural labourers who were persecuted during forced collectivization.

La Prensa Argentine newspaper brought under the control of the General Confederation of Labour.

La Semana Trágica The tragic week of January 1919 which saw violent clashes in Buenos Aires between different groups.

Ladies in White Cuban opposition group, formed in solidarity to those arrested in the Black Spring of 2003.

Landsberg Prison Gaol where Hitler was held for a short time after the Munich *Putsch*.

Laogai Prison camps in the People's Republic of China.

Latifundia A large plantation or estate in Cuba.

Latin America The countries of the Americas where Spanish or Portuguese is the main language.

League of German Maidens The girls' branch of the Hitler Youth.

Lebensborn The Nazi policy, run by Himmler, to increase birth rates as well as to adopt Aryan orphans during the war.

Lebensraum Meaning 'living space', part of the Nazi ideology that sought more territory for Germany.

Lend–Lease Act Passed in 1941 by the USA to supply its allies with goods, including military armaments, during the Second World War.

Lenin's Testament Written by Lenin; included criticism of Stalin's character. Luckily for Stalin it was not published.

Lessons of October Written by Trotsky in 1924 about the October Revolution; included criticisms of Kamenev and Zinoviev.

Liberator of the People Term used to describe Juan Perón.

Literary campaigns Cuban moves to promote literacy. A mass campaign was launched in 1961 to reach high levels of literacy.

Little Red Book Collection of Mao's sayings which were used as propaganda.

Long March Major retreat by Chinese Communists across China, 1934–5.

Glossary

Loyalty Day Celebrated on 17 October 1945, when Perón was released from prison.

Luftwaffe Germany's air force, which was under the command of Hermann Göring during the Nazi era.

Lushan Conference Chinese Communist Party conference in 1959 which included open criticism of Mao by Peng Dehuai.

M-26-7 Abbreviated name for the Cuban 26 July Movement.

Machismo Used in Latin America to describe 'manliness' or masculine pride, whereby men attempt to be dominant over women.

Magnitogorsk A Russian industrial city that was a prominent centre for iron and steel works during Stalin's Five-Year Plans.

Mariel Boatlift Migration of Cubans in 1980, when the port of Mariel was opened by Castro. The majority of the emigrants went to the USA.

Marriage Law Introduced by the Chinese Communist Party in 1950 to improve the legal rights of women in China.

Marshall Plan Set up by US President Harry Truman to provide economic assistance to countries recovering after the Second World War.

May 4th Movement Chinese protest movement against China's treatment in the 1919 Treaty of Versailles.

Mein Kampf *My Struggle*; a book written by Adolf Hitler, and published in 1925, outlining his ideological beliefs.

Mensheviks Political group active in the early twentieth century in Russia following socialist ideology; had differences from the Bolsheviks.

Military coup Overthrow of a government by military force.

Military Units to Aid Production (UMAPs) Cuban agricultural labour camps that were used to hold people, especially those described as 'social deviants'.

Moncada Barracks attack An assault by Fidel Castro on 26 July 1953 on a military stronghold of Fulgencio Batista.

Montoneros Militant, revolutionary wing of Perónists who were active in Argentina during the 1960s and 1970s.

Munich Agreement Agreement between Britain, Germany, France and Italy that allowed the annexation of the Sudetenland in Czechoslovakia.

Munich Putsch Attempted seizure of power by the NSDAP in November 1923; failed in its objectives.

Nanjing Decade Name given to the decade, 1927–37, when Nanjing was the capital of China.

Napolas Abbreviation for national political institutes of education, which were boarding schools for elite students during the Nazi era.

National Labour Force (RAD) A German workers' organization that sought to reduce unemployment; included the requirement for young men to complete national service for six months.

National Liberation Alliance (NLA) Paramilitary organization with far-right-wing beliefs that supported the police in repressing strikes in Argentina.

National Socialist German Workers' Party (NSDAP) Founded in 1920 and became known as the Nazi Party.

National Socialist Women's League Women's wing of the Nazi Party.

Navajos Youth group in Germany which opposed the Nazis, often by singing songs.

Naval blockade A sea blockade that restricts the movements of boats to a location. Used against Cuba during the missile crisis.

Nazi–Soviet Pact Defensive pact between the USSR and Germany signed in August 1939.

New Culture Movement Era in Chinese history that saw a number of intellectual developments including a rejection of traditional practices.

New Economic Policy (NEP) Economic policy introduced by Lenin in 1922. It relaxed War Communism, ended the requisition of crops and allowed for small levels of profit making, effectively lessening state control over the economy.

New Life Movement Social and cultural policy introduced by Chiang Kai-shek, advocating the importance of Confucian virtues.

New Plan Schacht's economic policies that sought to reduce the imbalance of trade and reduce unemployment.

Night of the Long Knives It led to a series of purges by the Nazis that sought to remove any opposition to their rule. This included a purge of the SA.

NKVD The People's Commissariat for Internal Affairs; the NKVD oversaw the police, prisons and secret police activities in the USSR.

Nomenklatura An elite group of party members in the USSR who held governmental positions.

Non-Aligned Movement Countries that did not align with major power blocs. This was notable during the Cold War when countries did not ally with either the USA or the USSR.

November Criminals Nickname given to the German politicians who signed the armistice ending the First World War.

Nuremberg Laws Discriminatory laws passed against Jewish people in Nazi Germany.

Octobrists A political group that sought to bring about moderate reform in Russia. They were supporters of constitutional monarchy.

Oligarchies Elite power holders in a society.

Operation Barbarossa Code name for the Nazi invasion of the USSR in 1941.

Opium Wars Fought in the nineteenth century between China and European powers.

Organization of Industry Set up by Hjalmar Schacht to increase the productivity of the German economy.

Orgburo Organizational bureau; the decision-making body of the Soviet government.

Oriente An area in the east of Cuba, generally poorer than provinces in the west.

Pampas Large grassland areas of Argentina, important for farming and rural industries.

Partido Laborista Argentine Labour Party that Juan Perón represented in the 1946 election.

Partido Ortodox Cuban Orthodox Party which followed socialism. Fidel Castro was a member.

Partido Perónista Argentine Justicialist Party founded by Juan Perón.

Patriarchal Male-dominated social order.

Patriotic Churches Churches that were allowed to operate in the People's Republic of China under Mao's rule but with state supervision.

Patronage Using power to control appointments and to ensure loyalty.

Peaceful coexistence Policy introduced by the Soviet Union to ease Cold War tensions with the USA.

People's Liberation Army (PLA) The army representing the Chinese Communist Party under the leadership of Mao Zedong.

People's Republic of China (PRC) Established in 1949 after the victory of the Chinese Communist Party.

Permanent Revolution Advocated by Leon Trotsky, informed the work of Comintern to encourage the development of communist parties and revolution around the world.

Perónist Youth Youth wing of the Argentine Perónist political party.

Pichón Racist term for a black Cuban.

Pingjin Campaign Successful series of campaigns launched by the People's Liberation Army during the latter stages of the Chinese Civil War in northern China.

Plantation A large area of land used for farming a single crop, such as sugar cane.

Platt Amendment Passed in 1901, it stipulated conditions for the USA to withdraw from Cuba.

Plaza de Mayo Large square in the centre of Buenos Aires, Argentina.

Plebiscite A vote on a change to a law by the electorate.

Poisonous Mushroom, The A Nazi anti-Semitic children's book published in 1938.

Politburo Policy-making committee of the Communist Party in both the Soviet Union and China.

Populist Appealing to the ordinary people in society.

Potsdam Conference July 1945 conference between the Grand Alliance to finalize plans for post-war Europe, especially Germany.

Pravda Truth: the official newspaper of the Communist Party of the Soviet Union.

Proletarian Referring to the working classes.

Proportional representation Electoral system that places the proportion of a vote in direct relation to the proportion of the seats. A fair system but often leads to coalition governments.

Provisional Government Temporary government of Russia between February and October 1917.

Proxy war When military powers use third parties to fight on their behalf.

Public works schemes Projects in Germany under the Nazi Party that sought to increase employment by building public works such as schools, roads and hospitals.

Purges Removal of political opposition.

Qing Dynasty A dynasty of China ruled by the Manchus, 1644–1911.

Radical Party Political party that held government in Argentina, 1916–30.

Radio Havana Launched in 1961, the government-controlled radio station of Cuba.

Rectification Policies introduced by Fidel Castro in the early 1970s in an attempt to improve the economy.

Rectification of Conduct Campaign Self-criticism campaign launched by Mao to promote ideological 'correctness'.

Red Army Army of the Chinese Communist Party, which later became the People's Liberation Army (PLA).

Red Guard Paramilitary youth group during the Cultural Revolution in China which carried out the attack on the 'four olds'.

Red Terror Period of repression and terror carried out by the Bolsheviks at the start of the Russian Civil War.

Reichkonkordat Mutual agreement between the Catholic Church and the Nazi Party, which was a commitment to non-interference.

Reichstag Democratically elected body of German government, which discussed and voted on laws.

Reichstag **Fire** Arson attack on the *Reichstag* building, carried out in February 1933.

Reparations Payments to be made for damages caused during war.

Glossary

Republic of the Children Theme park set up in Argentina by Eva Perón.

Reunification Campaigns Operations by the Chinese Communist Party to secure borders and bring regions of China under centralized control.

Revolution Betrayed, The A book by the exiled Leon Trotsky, published in 1937, which criticized Stalin's leadership of the USSR.

Revolutionary correctness The Chinese Communist Party's policy of encouraging strict adherence to its ideology.

Rhineland An area that was demilitarized under the terms of the Treaty of Versailles. This was overturned in 1936 when German troops were sent into the region.

Rise and Fall of the Third Reich, The A book by William Shirer, published in 1960, detailing the history of Nazi Germany.

Roca–Runciman Agreement Trading agreement between Britain and Argentina in 1933.

Russian Civil War Conflict between the Reds and Whites, which helped the communists to consolidate their control.

Russian Orthodox Church The main religion in Russia, repressed at different times by the government.

Russification Policy of making Russian language and culture dominant throughout the country.

Ryutin Affair Opposition action against Stalin in 1932, especially focused on Martemyan Ryutin's criticism of collectivization policies.

Saarland Area in south-west Germany that was under French control which voted to rejoin Germany in 1935.

Sáenz Peña electoral reform law Passed in 1912 and gave men the vote in Argentina.

San Juan earthquake Severe earthquake that hit Argentina in 1944.

Sandinistas Members of the left-wing political group, the Sandinista National Liberation Front, which took power in Nicaragua in 1979.

Schutzstaffel **(SS)** 'Protection squadron': a Nazi paramilitary organization that ran security, surveillance, police forces and the concentration camps under the leadership of Heinrich Himmler.

Second Sino-Japanese War War between China and Japan, 1937–45.

Secret Speech Made by Khrushchev in 1956, it was critical of Stalinist policies including the purges and the cult of personality.

Secretariat Administrative body of the Soviet government.

Show trials Public trials in the USSR.

Sierra Cristal Mountainous area in the east of Cuba.

Sierra Maestra Mountain range in Cuba. The base for the 26 July Movement from 1957 to 1958.

Sino-American Rapprochement Name given to the improved relations between China and the USA during the 1970s.

Sino-Soviet Treaty of Friendship, Alliance and Mutual Assistance Signed in 1950 between Mao and Stalin, it laid the foundations for economic assistance from the USSR to China during the first Five-Year Plan.

Smoot–Hawley Tariff Act Passed in 1930, it increased tariffs on goods imported into the USA.

Social Democratic Party (SPD) Left-wing political party in Germany.

Socialism in One Country Stalinist ideological position that advocated the development of the USSR as a priority rather than the spreading of revolution to other states in the world.

Socialist realism Method for promoting socialist values in artwork.

Socialist Revolutionaries Supporters of the February Revolution; some members eventually joined the Bolsheviks.

Society of Argentinian Writers (SADE) Society representing the interests of writers and artists in Argentina.

Sonderweg Meaning 'special path', a historiographical theory which places Nazism as a likely result of Germany's unique history.

Sovietization of Eastern Europe States in Eastern Europe adopting communist governments with Soviet encouragement.

Spanish Civil War Civil war in Spain, 1936–9, which involved additional European powers, for example Nazi Germany supported Franco.

Spanish–American War War fought between Spain and the USA in 1898, which led to Cuban independence from Spain.

Spartacist Uprising Strike and civil unrest in 1919 during the German revolution caused by communists.

Spartacists Communist group whose leaders were Karl Liebknecht and Rosa Luxemburg.

Speak Bitterness Opportunities for Chinese agricultural labourers to speak out against former landlords.

Special Period The time after the end of the Cold War when Cuba found itself isolated and experienced difficult economic conditions.

Spiritual Chief of the Nation Term used to describe Eva Perón in schools.

Stab in the back myth A myth circulated in Germany after the First World War that the army was betrayed by people at home and those who signed the armistice.

Stagnation In economic terms, this refers to a lack of economic growth and modernization. This was the problem for the Soviet Union and Eastern European satellite states during the 1970s and 1980s.

Strength Through Joy State-run organization in Nazi Germany that arranged leisure opportunities for workers, including day trips, cruises, hiking and trips to the library.

***Sturmabteilung* (SA)** 'Storm battalion': a paramilitary wing of the Nazi Party led by Ernst Röhm until 1934, when it was purged.

Sudetenland An area of Czechoslovakia that was ceded to Germany after the Munich Conference.

Surplus Excess production.

Süss the Jew A Nazi anti-Semitic film made in 1940.

Swing Youth Youth groups in Germany who rebelled against the state, especially by listening to banned jazz or swing music.

Syndicalism Movement that seeks to increase the power and influence of trade unions.

Syndicate Organization that represents several interest groups.

Taiwan Straits Crisis Conflict and tension between the People's Republic of China, Taiwan and the USA over disputed islands.

Ten-Million Ton Harvest Target set by Fidel Castro to give the Cuban sugar industry a boost on a national level; he wanted the country to hit 10 million tons in the harvest of 1970.

Third Way Self-described term for Perón's ideology, policies that sought to be neither communist nor capitalist. Can be viewed in the context of the Cold War.

Three Principles of the People Ideological roots of the Guomindang. The principles refer to democracy, nationalism and people's livelihood.

Towards a Better Future A radio broadcast by Eva Perón which focused on the needs of the Argentine people.

Trans-Siberian Railway Railway built across Russia connecting Moscow to Vladivostok.

Treaty of Brest-Litovsk Peace Treaty between Russia and Germany signed in March 1918 by the Bolshevik Party.

Treaty of Versailles Signed during the Paris Peace Conference in 1919, this provided the details for the treatment of Germany after the First World War.

Triple A The Argentine Anti-Communist Alliance, a death squad led by Rega.

Triumph of the Will A 1935 film directed by Leni Riefenstahl celebrating the achievements of the Nazi state.

Uighur, Hui and Kirghiz Minority ethnic groups in China.

United Officers' Group (GOU) Faction of the Argentine military responsible for the 1943 military coup. Perón was a member of this faction.

Usury Placing very high levels of interest on loans.

Vanguard party Part of Lenin's adaption of Marxism, which advocated the need for a political group to lead the revolution, to create a dictatorship of the proletariat.

Vietnam War Major Cold War conflict. The People's Republic of China supported Ho Chi Minh and the North Vietnamese.

Volksgemeinschaft German term meaning 'people's community'; used by the Nazis to describe their aims for society.

Wall Street Crash Collapse of share prices on the New York Stock Exchange in 1929; trigger of the economic depression.

Wannsee Conference Meeting of Nazi ministers and SS officers to decide on the fate of Jewish people in Europe, essentially beginning the Holocaust.

War Communism Economic policy during the Russian Civil War that involved the requisitioning of crops to support the war effort.

Warlord era China between 1916 and 1927, when regional warlords held control over different parts of the country.

Weimar Republic The German government between 1918 and 1934, named after the town of Weimar.

White Rose A group opposing the Nazis, led by Hans and Sophie Scholl. It provided moral opposition to inhumane policies carried out in Germany at the time, for example the euthanasia programme.

Women's Perónist Political Party Set up by Eva Perón to advance women's rights in Argentina.

Xinhai Revolution The 1911–12 revolution in China that ended dynastic rule.

Xinjiang Province A province in western China with a large Muslim population.

Yalta Conference February 1945 conference between the Grand Alliance to make decisions about the reorganization of Europe after the Second World War.

Yanan Area of Chinese Communist Party control in northern China after the Long March.

Key figures

Allende, Salvador (1908–73) Former president of Chile who was overthrown in 1973 by a military coup. He was a Marxist and an ally of Fidel Castro.

Alvear, Marcelo (1868–1942) President of Argentina, 1922–8. Member of the Radical Party.

Aramburu, Pedro (1903–70) Argentine army general who was involved in the 1955 overthrow of Perón. Aramburu was kidnapped and murdered by the Montoneros.

Árbenz, Jacobo (1913–71) Democratically elected president of Guatemala who was ousted from power in 1954 by a coup that was backed by the CIA.

Arenas, Reinaldo (1943–90) Cuban writer and author of *Before Night Falls*, which details some of the homophobia in Cuba.

Batista, Fulgencio (1901–73) Military dictator of Cuba, 1952–9.

Bonhoeffer, Dietrich (1906–45) German theologian and vocal opponent of the Nazis, including the persecution of Jewish people. He was arrested during the war and later executed.

Borges, Jorge Luis (1899–1986) Argentine writer, public figure and critic of the Peróns.

Brezhnev, Leonid (1906–82) Soviet leader after Khrushchev.

Brüning, Heinrich (1885–1970) German chancellor 1930–2 and a member of the Catholic Centre Party.

Bukharin, Nikolai (1888–1938) Prominent member of the Communist Party of the Soviet Union, a supporter of the New Economic Policy and Socialism in One Country. He was ousted by Stalin in 1929 due to his opposition to collectivization. Bukharin was executed in 1938 after a show trial.

Cámpora, Héctor (1909–80) Argentine politician and left-wing Perónist whose presidency in 1973 paved the way for the return of Juan Perón to office.

Carter, James 'Jimmy' (1924–) President of the USA, 1977–81.

Castillo, Rámon (1873–1944) President of Argentina at the time of the 1943 military coup by the United Officers' Group (GOU).

Castro, Fidel (1926–2016) Revolutionary leader of Cuba, 1959–2008.

Castro, Raúl (1931–) Brother of Fidel and one of the leaders of the 26 July Movement. He became Cuba's president in 2008 after Fidel retired.

Chen Duxiu (1879–1942) Founding member of the Chinese Communist Party who was influential during the New Culture Movement.

Chiang Kai-shek (1887–1975) Leader of the Guomindang and the Republic of China.

Deng Xiaoping (1904–97) Important Chinese Communist Party leader who was purged during the Cultural Revolution but later became paramount leader of China.

Drexler, Anton (1884–1942) Founder of the German Workers' Party.

Duarte, Eva María (1919–52) Argentine actress, social welfare activist and wife of Juan Perón.

Ebert, Friedrich (1871–1925) Member of the Social Democratic Party of Germany; first president of the Weimar Republic.

Eichmann, Adolf (1906–62) High-ranking Nazi who was one of the organizers of the Holocaust; managed to escape to Argentina after the Second World War but was later captured, put on trial and hanged.

Espín, Vilma (1930–2007) Cuban revolutionary who was a prominent leader of the Cuban Women's Federation (FMC) and one of the authors of the 1975 Family Code.

Farrell, Edelmiro (1887–1980) President of Argentina who appointed Perón to the position of vice-president in January 1944.

Gay, Luis (1903–88) Argentine trade union leader who opposed Perón's reorganization of trade unions.

Goebbels, Joseph (1879–1945) Head of the Nazi Ministry of Propaganda, co-ordinated the wide range of propaganda measures visible in the Nazi state.

Göring, Hermann (1893–1946) Influential and high-ranking Nazi who was the commander-in-chief of the Luftwaffe and minister of economics put in charge of the Four-Year Plan.

Guevara, Ernesto 'Che' (1928–67) Argentine-born revolutionary who worked to promote Marxism and independence movements around the world. Played a major role in the Cuban revolution.

Himmler, Heinrich (1900–45) Leading Nazi politician and head of the SS.

Hitler, Adolf (1889–1945) Leader of Germany, 1933–45.

Kamenev, Lev (1883–1936) A Soviet politician who worked with Zinoviev and Trotsky in the United Opposition to Stalin. He was executed after a show trial in 1936.

Kennedy, John F. (1917–63) President of the USA, 1961–3.

Khrushchev, Nikita (1894–1971) Leader of the Soviet Union, 1953–64.

Kim Il-Sung (1912–94) North Korean dictator, 1948–94.

Kirov, Sergei (1886–1934) A leading member of the Communist Party of the Soviet Union who was killed in the Smolny Institute in 1934, triggering a wave of political purges in the USSR.

Lenin, Vladimir (1870–1924) Led the Bolsheviks in the October Revolution, and under his leadership set up the USSR.

Li Dazhao (1888–1927) Founding member of the Chinese Communist Party. He died during the Shanghai Massacre in 1927.

Lichtenberg, Bernhard (1875–1943) Opponent and critic of the Nazis who publicly protested about the treatment of Jewish people in Germany.

Liu Shaoqi (1898–1969) Leading member of the Chinese Communist Party who was purged during the Cultural Revolution.

Lonardi, Eduardo (1896–1956) Argentine soldier who led the overthrow of Perón in 1955.

López Rega, José (1916–89) Argentine politician and right-wing Perónist who was behind the repression and purge of the left-wing factions.

Ludendorff, Erich (1865–1937) Influential German general who supported both the Kapp *Putsch* and the Munich *Putsch*.

Mao Zedong (1893–1976) Leader of the People's Republic of China, 1949–76.

Marshall, Niní (1903–96) Argentine comic actress whose work was criticized under the Argentine governments of the 1940s.

Martí, José (1853–95) Cuban writer and independence movement leader. Had a major influence on Fidel Castro.

Marx, Karl (1818–83) German political theorist whose writings developed the idea of communism.

Matos, Huber (1918–2014) Former member of Cuba's 26 July Movement, he was imprisoned for twenty years after criticizing the move towards Marxism once the movement had gained power.

Mengele, Josef (1911–79) German SS officer and doctor who escaped to Argentina after the Second World War. He was involved in human experimentation during the war. He was never captured.

Mercante, Domingo (1898–1976) Argentine military officer, politician and member of the United Officers' Group (GOU). An ally of Perón who worked with him on passing different reforms for the workers in Argentina.

Meyerhold, Vsevolod (1874–1940) Russian theatre director and producer who was purged during the Great Terror, leading to his execution.

Mommsen, Hans (1930–2015) German historian who first put forward the theory that Hitler was a weak dictator.

Moore, Carlos (1942–) Cuban writer and critic of Castro who argued that conditions for black Cubans did not improve under Castro's rule.

Mukhina, Vera (1889–1953) Soviet sculptor whose most famous work is the sculpture *Worker and Kolkhoz Woman*.

Mussolini, Benito (1883–1945) Leader of the Italian Fascist Party and ruler of Italy, 1922–43.

Nicholas II (1868–1918) Last tsar of the Russian Empire, abdicated in 1917.

Niemöller, Martin (1892–1984) German theologian, founder of the Confessing Church and opponent of the Nazis. He wrote the famous sermon 'First they came for the Socialists …'.

Nixon, Richard (1913–94) President of USA 1969–74 who was associated with the improved relationship with the People's Republic of China.

Ostrovsky, Nikolai (1904–36) Soviet socialist realist writer who wrote *How the Steel was Tempered*.

Peng Dehuai (1898–1974) Senior member of the Chinese Communist Party who was critical of Mao over the Great Leap Forward and subsequent famine.

Perón, Isabel Martínez de (1931–) Argentine-born wife of Juan Perón who became vice-president in 1973 and later president after the death of her husband.

Perón, Juan (1895–1974) Three-time president of Argentina.

Pugliese, Osvaldo (1905–95) Argentine tango pianist who fell out of favour with Juan Perón.

Reyes, Cipriano (1906–2001) Argentine union leader who opposed Perón's reorganization of trade unions.

Riefenstahl, Leni (1902–2003) German film director and photographer.

Röhm, Ernst (1887–1934) German military officer and founder of the SA. Killed during the Night of the Long Knives.

Rust, Bernhard (1883–1945) Nazi education minister.

Rykov, Alexei (1881–1938) Russian revolutionary who was executed after the Trial of the Twenty One in 1938 along with Bukharin. A former member of the right opposition to Stalin.

Sánchez, Celia (1920–80) Key figure in the Cuban revolution.

Saslavsky, Luis (1903–95) Argentine film director.

Schacht, Hjalmar (1877–1970) Germany's minister of economics, 1934–7.

Scholl, Hans (1918–43) Joint leader with his sister, Sophie, of the White Rose opposition group in Munich.

Scholl, Sophie (1921–43) Joint leader with her brother, Hans, of the White Rose opposition group in Munich.

Key figures

Solzhenitsyn, Aleksandr (1918–2008) Russian novelist and historian who spent time in Soviet *gulags* after the Second World War. He later wrote *The Gulag Archipelago*.

Speer, Albert (1905–81) Nazi architect and minister of armaments and war production during the Second World War.

Stakhanov, Aleksei (1906–77) Model worker in the USSR who mined record amounts of coal. Gave his name to the Stakhanovite Movement, where workers tried to emulate very high production levels.

Stalin, Joseph (1878–1953) Authoritarian leader of the USSR, 1929–53.

Strasser, Gregor (1892–1934) Influential member of the Nazi Party during its rise to power, who had a number of disagreements with Hitler. Killed during the Night of the Long Knives.

Strasser, Otto (1897–1974) German politician who broke away from Hitler to form a left-wing faction of the Nazi Party alongside his brother Gregor.

Stresemann, Gustav (1878–1929) Notable German politician who negotiated improved economic conditions and international relations during the Weimar era.

Sun Yat-sen (1866–1925) Chinese revolutionary and original leader of the Guomindang.

Tomsky, Mikhail (1880–1936) Russian politician who allied with Bukharin in opposition to Stalin. He did not hold a significant political position under Stalin's rule and was targeted for arrest during the purges. He died by suicide.

Trotsky, Leon (1879–1940) Influential member of the Communist Party of the Soviet Union. He played a key role in the Russian Civil War and held strong ideological beliefs.

Trujilo, Rafael (1891–1961) Dictator in the Dominican Republic; ruled the country between 1930 and 1961.

Valladares, Armando (1937–) Cuban writer who was arrested and imprisoned by Castro's regime. An outspoken critic who wrote books detailing the human rights abuses that took place in Cuba after the 26 July Movement had taken power.

van der Lubbe, Marinus (1909–34) Dutch communist who was arrested and executed for the *Reichstag* Fire.

von Galen, Clemens (1878–1946) Cardinal of the German Catholic Church and critic of the Nazi regime. He spoke out against some Nazi policies.

von Hindenburg, Paul (1847–1934) German military officer and president of the Weimar Republic from 1925 until his death.

von Papen, Franz (1879–1969) Chancellor of Germany in 1932 who later recommended the appointment of Hitler as chancellor.

von Schirach, Baldur (1907–74) Nazi minister in charge of the Hitler Youth.

von Schleicher, Kurt (1882–1934) Final chancellor of Weimar Germany.

von Stauffenberg, Claus (1907–44) German army officer who attempted to assassinate Hitler.

Yao Wenyuan (1931–2005) Chinese politician, literary critic and a member of the Gang of Four who wrote a criticism of the play *The Dismissal of Hai Rui From Office*.

Yrigoyen, Hipólito (1852–1933) President of Argentina 1916–22 and 1928–30. Member of the Radical Party. Overthrown in the 1930 military coup.

Yuan Shikai (1859–1916) President of the Republic of China between 1912 and 1916.

Zhou Enlai (1898–1976) Leading member of the Chinese Communist Party in the twentieth century.

Zinoviev, Grigory (1883–1936) Soviet politician, head of Comintern and member of the United Opposition. Purged and was put on trial in 1936, leading to his execution.

Timeline

The USSR under Joseph Stalin, 1924–53

The establishment of the Soviet Union and the rise to power of Joseph Stalin

1914–17	Russia was involved in the First World War. Tsarist rule was increasingly unpopular as a result of the war
1917	The February Revolution ended tsarist rule. Nicholas II abdicated
	The October Revolution brought the Bolshevik Party into power
1918–22	The Russian Civil War between the Reds, Whites and Greens. The Reds won
1922	The Union of Soviet Socialist Republics (USSR) was officially established
	Treaty of Rapallo with Germany
1924	Lenin died; he was responsible for setting up the early political systems and structures of the USSR
	USSR officially recognized as a state by Britain and France
1924–9	Political struggle within the Communist Party of the Soviet Union (CPSU); there was a division between the left and right wings of the party and Stalin emerged as the unchallenged leader by 1929

Foreign policy events under Stalin

1926	Treaty of Berlin with Germany
1928	Comintern initiatives divided the left wing in Germany
1934	Trade agreement with Germany
	USSR joined the League of Nations
1935	Security agreements with France and Czechoslovakia
1936	Anti-Comintern Pact between Germany and Japan
1936–9	USSR supported the international brigades in the Spanish Civil War
1938	Munich Agreement
1939	Signing of the Nazi–Soviet Pact followed by the invasion of Poland
1941	Nazi Germany attacked the USSR in Operation Barbarossa

Germany under Adolf Hitler, 1933–45

Events leading to Hitler's rise to power

1918	Nov: Surrender of German military brought an end to the First World War
1919	June: The Treaty of Versailles was signed between Germany and the Allied powers
	Aug: Publication of the Weimar constitution which set up the political structure and systems for governing Germany. This brought an end to the revolutionary period after the war
	Sept: Hitler joined the German Workers' Party (DAP), beginning his political life
1920	Feb: DAP renamed as the National Socialist German Workers' Party (NSDAP). Ideology of Nazism developed
1923	Nov: Munich *Putsch* was an attempt by the NSDAP to seize power. It failed, resulting in Hitler's imprisonment when he wrote *Mein Kampf*
1929	Wall Street Crash led to global economic depression. Germany was badly hit, leading to high unemployment
1933	Jan: Hitler appointed as chancellor

China under Mao Zedong, 1949–76

Events leading to the establishment of the People's Republic of China under Mao Zedong

1911–12	Opposition to the rule of the Qing Dynasty eventually led to the Xinhai Revolution; end of dynastic rule
1912–16	Short-lived Republic of China under the rule of President Yuan Shikai
1916–27	China fragmented into regional power centres; this is known as the Warlord Era
1927–37	Chiang Kai-shek established control over large areas of China with a Nationalist government; known as the Nanjing Decade
1937–45	The Second Sino-Japanese War between China and Japan. This became part of the wider world war after 1941 when the USA entered
1946–9	The Chinese Civil War fought between the communists and the nationalists. The communists won; Mao was the leader of the People's Republic of China (PRC)

Timeline

Foreign policy events under Mao Zedong

1950–3	Korean War. The PRC supported North Korea in its war against South Korea and the United Nations (dominated by the USA)
1954–5	Taiwan Straits Crisis: dispute over islands close to Taiwan
1955–75	Vietnam War: PRC provided support to Ho Chi Minh and the North Vietnamese
1962	Sino-Indian border war
1969	Sino-Soviet border conflict

Cuba under Fidel Castro, 1959–2006

Events leading to Fidel Castro's rise to power

1898	Spanish–American War led to Cuban independence but with a dependent relationship on the USA
1901	Platt Amendment stipulated conditions by the USA for Cuban independence which were added to the constitution
1926	Fidel Castro was born
1952	March: Fulgencio Batista seized power in a military coup and created a dictatorship
1953	July: Moncada Barracks attack by Castro and his supporters
	Oct: Trial of Fidel Castro leading to him being sentenced to prison
1954	Batista dissolved the Cuban Parliament
1955	May: Castro was released from prison; he formed the 26 July Movement
	Castro and his brother, Raúl, met Ernesto 'Che' Guevara in Mexico City
1956	Dec: *Granma* expedition from Mexico to Cuba
1957–8	Guerrilla attacks by Castro and revolutionary groups against Batista; they were based in the Sierra Maestra mountains
1959	Jan: Batista fled Cuba
	Feb: Castro became premier of Cuba

Argentina under Juan Perón, 1946–74

Events for Juan Peron's rise to power

1810–18	Argentine War of Independence against Spain
1895	Juan Perón was born in Lobos, Buenos Aires province of Argentina
1919	Jan: *La Semana Trágica*, the tragic week which saw unrest, riots and a breakdown of order in Buenos Aires
1930	Sept: Argentine *coup d'état* by the military led to the overthrow of the Radical Party leader Hipólito Yrigoyen
Early 1930s	Argentina was affected by economic depression
1930–43	The Decade of Infamy
1933	May: Roca–Runciman Agreement between Argentina and Britain
1943	June: Military coup by the United Officers' Group (GOU) that led to the establishment of a military *junta* in Argentina
	Dec: Juan Perón was appointed minister of labour in the new government
1944	Jan: San Juan earthquake in Argentina. Juan Perón met Eva Maria Duarte and they later married
	Jan: Perón was appointed vice-president of Argentina
1945	Oct: Perón was forced to resign by political opposition and was arrested and placed in prison. He was quickly released due to overwhelming opposition
1946	Feb: Perón was elected president of Argentina, representing at the time the *Partido Laborista*

Answers

1: Authoritarian states

Page 9, Understanding terminology

Term	Definition
Consolidation	Methods used to secure power once an authoritarian state has been created
Legal methods	Often political measures to establish and maintain power through the use of laws. These could include writing constitutions
Social division	Refers to discontent or inequality in society
Ideology	A set of guiding ideas that are used by individuals and political parties. This includes fascism
Foreign policy	Policy measures outside a state including alliances, trade deals and military engagements
Charismatic leadership	Method used to ensure conformity to the rule of a leader. This often involves the development of a cult of personality
Minorities	Groups in societies that are not dominant. They may experience repression or more inequality under specific authoritarian states. For example, religious groups and different ethnic groups

2: The USSR under Joseph Stalin, 1924–53

Page 15, Stalin, Trotsky or Lenin?

Example	Lenin?	Stalin?	Trotsky?	Significance?
Proposed Socialism in One Country as an ideological position on revolution		✗		
Made the decision to introduce the NEP after the Russian Civil War	✗			
Proposed the need for a vanguard party to lead the revolution and build a socialist state	✗			
Played a crucial role in both the October Revolution and the Russian Civil War			✗	
Held positions of power that allowed him to place supporters into the party		✗		
Was against both the NEP and Socialism in One Country			✗	

Page 17, Chronology activity

Year	Event
1924 (May)	Lenin's Testament not being read out to the members of the CPSU
1924 (October)	Trotsky criticized Kamenev and Zinoviev in his Lessons of October
1926	The formation of the united opposition of Trotsky, Kamenev and Zinoviev against Stalin and the right wing of the party
1927	Expulsion of Trotsky, Kamenev and Zinoviev from the party after accusations of factionalism
1928	Stalin's backing away from the NEP and launching an attack on Bukharin and the right wing of the party
1929	Stalin was seen as the clear frontrunner for the Soviet leadership

Answers

Page 23, The role of propaganda

Example of propaganda	Explanation of significance
Poster showing Stalin steering a ship with the flag of the USSR in the background	• Role of Stalin as leader • Unity of the Soviet Union
A painting showing a group of farm workers eating food together. The painting is called *A Collective Farm Feast*	• Promoting policy of collectivization • Celebrating the achievements of workers
A photograph of Lenin addressing troops in 1920. Both Trotsky and Kamenev have been edited out of the picture	• Reinforcing the cult of personality of Lenin • Reducing Trotsky and Kamenev's historical importance
A sculpture called *Worker and Kolkhoz Woman* (see Source 10)	• Role of both men and women in building the socialist state • Celebrating workers
A book called *Energy* by Feodor Gladkov, published in 1932, that tells of the heroism of a group of construction workers	• Socialist realism that is written for the majority of the people to understand • Celebrating the important role of workers in industrialization

Page 25, Eliminate irrelevance

Foreign policy plays a crucial role in the maintenance of power for authoritarian states. ~~Even in the twenty-first century we can see that successful foreign policies can have a positive impact on how different countries fare.~~ Stalin's foreign policy had different priorities at different stages of his leadership over the USSR. Early on, with the policies of industrialization and collectivization, Stalin prioritized domestic development rather than an expansionist foreign policy. ~~Factories were built across the Soviet Union and a major focus was on the development of heavy industry.~~ However as fascism became increasing popular across Europe, Stalin increasingly realized the need for collective security and sought stronger alliances.

3: Germany under Adolf Hitler, 1933–45

Page 33, Political structure of Weimar

	Role 1	Role 2	Role 3
The voters	All men and women over the age of twenty	They vote for the president every seven years	They vote for the *Reichstag* every four years
The president	Appoints and dismisses the chancellor	Controls the armed forces	Can use Article 48 to pass emergency laws
The chancellor and ministers	Runs the government offices	Proposes new laws to the *Reichstag*	
The *Reichstag*	Is democratically elected	Seat holders are called deputies	They vote on laws
The *Reichsrat*	Can advise the chancellor on the passing of new laws	Has the power of veto over the introduction of new laws	

4: China under Mao Zedong, 1949–76

Page 65, Conditions or methods?

Event	Conditions?	Methods?
Land reform in Jiangxi Province		✗
Guerrilla warfare tactics		✗
Hyperinflation in China during the 1940s	✗	
The New Culture Movement	✗	
Mao's adaptation of Marxism–Leninism		✗
High levels of poverty in China, majority of population were agricultural labourers	✗	
Code of Conduct for the Red Army		✗
Growing unpopularity of GMD leadership	✗	
Mao's military strategy during the civil war		✗
Rectification campaigns		✗
Treatment of landlords by the CCP		✗
Failure of early Chinese Republic and the warlord era	✗	

5: Cuba under Fidel Castro, 1959–2006

Page 91, Match the terms to the descriptions

Term	Definition
Institute of Agrarian Reform	An organization set up to oversee the land reform policies after the Agrarian Reform Law of 1959
Latifundias	Large areas of land, usually taking the form of a plantation. These were limited under Castro's agrarian reforms
Diversification	Policy which sought to reduce Cuba's reliance on sugar by developing other domestic industries
Ten-Million Ton Harvest	National target, proclaimed by Fidel Castro, to be achieved in 1970.

6: Argentina under Juan Perón, 1946–74

Page 105, Eliminate irrelevance

Economic conditions were of significance to Perón's rise to power. Argentina had been affected, like many countries (such as Germany), by the economic depression. The depression led to increased unemployment and a restricted international trading market which was a problem for the Argentine export economy. At this point, the USA had introduced the New Deal as a method to deal with the economic problems it was experiencing. Further, the depression increased levels of nationalism, especially in relation to the reactions to the Roca–Runciman Agreement of 1933, which was seen to favour British interests.

Text with pink highlighting could be seen to be less relevant. Text with yellow highlighting could be explained in more detail.

Acknowledgements

The Publishers would like to thank the following for permission to reproduce copyright material:
German Propaganda Archive (http://research.calvin.edu/german-propaganda-archive/unser36.htm). *South China Morning Post*, Richard Wong, (www.scmp.com/business/article/2052134/cubas-sugar-exports-help-explain-rise-fidel-castro). *The Militant* (www.themilitant.com/1996/603/603_25.html). Thedailybell.com (www.thedailybell.com/editorials/richard-ebeling-chinas-great-inflation-helped-bring-the-communists-to-power/). United States Holocaust Memorial Museum, 'Women in the Third Reich', Holocaust Encyclopedia (www.ushmm.org/wlc/en/article.php?ModuleId=10005205).

Acknowledgements: American Presidency Project, Gerhard Peters and John T. Woolley (www.presidency.ucsb.edu/ws/?pid=58824). André Deutsch, Franz von Papen, *Memoirs*, 1952. Avalon Project, Harvard Law School (http://avalon.law.yale.edu/imt/partiv.asp). Bantam Books, Fox Butterfield, *China: Alive in the Bitter Sea*, 1990. BBC Books, Laurence Rees, *The Nazis: A Warning From History*, 2003. Black House Publishing, Kerry Bolton, *Perón and Perónism*, 2014. Encounter Books, Armando Valladares, *Against All Hope: A Memoir of Life in Castro's Gulag*, 2001. Foreign Languages Press, David L. Weitzman, *Mao Tse-tung and The Chinese Revolution*, 1953. Fourth International (www.marxists.org/history/etol/newspape/fi/vol04/no07/phelan.htm). Heinemann, Geoff Stewart, *China 1900–76*, 2006. Hodder Arnold, P.D. Allan, *Russia and Eastern Europe*, 1983. Hodder Education, David Evans and Jane Jenkins, *Years of Russia, the USSR and the Collapse of Soviet Communism*, 2008; Geoff Layton, *Germany: The Third Reich 1933–45*, 2005; John Hite and Chris Hinton, *Weimar and Nazi Germany*, 2000; Michael Lynch, *Access to History for the IB Diploma: Authoritarian states*, second edition, 2015; Michael Lynch, *Bolshevik and Stalinist Russia: 1917–64*, 2015. Hodder & Stoughton, Michael Lynch, *The People's Republic of China Since 1949*, 1998. Marxists Internet Archive (www.marxists.org/history/cuba/archive/castro/1961/04/23.htm; www.marxists.org/archive/trotsky/germany/elect.htm; www.marxists.org/history/argentina/montoneros/introduction.htm; www.marxists.org/history/argentina/peron/1951/speech.htm; www.marxists.org/history/cuba/archive/castro/1953/10/16.htm). National Archives, *Magazine of The Friends of The National Archives*, Vol. 23, No. 1, April 2012. New York Labor News Co., Karl Marx and Friedrich Engels, *Manifesto of the Communist Party*, 1908. Office of the Secretary of Defense, Jacques Rossi, *The Gulag Handbook: An Historical Dictionary of Soviet Penitentiary Institutions and Terms Related to the Forced Labor Camps*, 1985. Office of the United States Chief Counsel for Prosecution of Axis Criminality, *Nazi Conspiracy and Aggression Volume IV*, 1946. Oxford University Press, R. Keith Schoppa, *Twentieth Century China: A History in Documents*, 2011. Pathfinder Press, Elizabeth Stone editor, *Women and the Cuban Revolution: Speeches and Documents by Fidel Castro, Vilma Espín and others*, 1981. Penguin, Edwin Williamson, *The Penguin History of Latin America*, 1992. Presidencia de La Nación, Subsecretaría de Informaciones, Juan Perón, *Perónist Doctrine*, Buenos Aires, 1952. Progress Publishers, Vladimir Lenin, *Imperialism, The Highest Stage of Capitalism*, 1916. Red Letter Press, Leon Trotsky, *The Permanent Revolution & Results and Prospects*, 2010. Routledge, Anthony Wood, *The Russian Revolution*, second edition, 1986. Secker & Warberg, William Shirer, *The Rise and Fall of the Third Reich*, 1960. Translating Cuba, Yoani Sanchez (http://translatingcuba.com/cdr-citizen-representation-or-political-control-yoani-sanchez/). University of Exeter Press, J. Noakes and G. Pridham, editors, *Nazism, 1919–45*, volume 2, 1984. University of Florida, George A. Smathers Libraries (http://ufdc.ufl.edu/AA00021904/00001/11j). Vintage Books, Jung Chang and Jon Halliday, *Mao: The Unknown Story*, 2007. Yad Vashem/Pergamon Press, Y. Arad, Y. Gutman and A. Margaliot, *Documents on the Holocaust: Selected Sources on the Destruction of the Jews of Germany and Austria, Poland, and the Soviet Union*, 1981. Yale University Press, Detlev J.K. Peukert, *Inside Nazi Germany*, translated by Richard Deveson, 1987.

Photo credits: p19 Hulton Archive/Getty Images; **p25** Tim Wainwright/Alamy Stock Photo; **p30t** Public domain via Wikipedia; **p45l** Keystone/Getty Images; **p45r** Keystone/Getty Images; **p49** Bettmann via Getty Images; **p51** Universal History Archive/UIG via Getty Images; **p65** Sovfoto/UIG via Getty Images; **pp70, 75** Stefan R. Landsberger Collection, International Institute of Social History (Amsterdam); **p79** Granger Historical Picture Archive/Alamy Stock Photo; **p80** Mark Kauffman/The LIFE Picture Collection/Getty Images; **p83l** Library of Congress, LC-DIG-ppmsc-03256; **p83m** ITAR-TASS News Agency/Alamy Stock Photo; **p83r** Getty Images; **p85** Kevin Foy/Alamy Stock Photo; **p89** TASS via Getty Images; **p93** Lee Lockwood/The LIFE Images Collection/Getty Images; **p113** Public domain via Wikipedia; **p117** Keystone Pictures USA/Alamy Stock Photo.

Every effort has been made to trace all copyright holders, but if any have been inadvertently overlooked, the Publishers will be pleased to make the necessary arrangements at the first opportunity.

Notes

Notes